PSYCHIC ADVENTURES and the UNSEEN WORLD

by Clare A. Clark

PSYCHIC ADVENTURES and the UNSEEN WORLD

CLARE A. CLARK

Valkyrie
Press, Inc.

International Standard Book Number — 0-912760-33-8
Library of Congress Catalog Card Number — 76-42918

First Printing

PUBLISHERS

Valkyrie
Press, Inc.

2135 1st Avenue South
St. Petersburg, Florida 33712

1996777

*To my husband and sons
who have had so much
patience with my endeavors.*

TABLE OF CONTENTS

PSYCHIC
ADVENTURES
and the
UNSEEN WORLD

by Clare A. Clark

L'ife never ends, nor do our spiritually attained psychic abilities. The recognition of the latter began with ancient civilizations; and "psi" has emerged now and then, as a butterfly comes out of the cocoon, lives briefly, and dies. But another coiled creature carries on in the same tradition; spins its casing, and lies inert for a while, until the time arrives for its awakening and changing into a more beautiful being.

Once again we are witnessing the extrusion of the chrysalis of our innermost natures. The children of the Aquarian Age will be the new leaders. We older ones will have to be the teachers. Many of us possess this ability, but do not know it . . . will not accept it. However, we must learn more about our natural inheritance, so we can lead this generation from the world of drugs to the easier-to-turn-on reality of self-knowledge.

With a little practice in the methods of relaxing, breathing, meditating, and focusing attention, we can show them how to reach their inner senses so they can bring out the illuminating images that can arise from their own souls. It is something they have within, that they can give birth to all by themselves. No chemical substances are needed to unfold the perfections of the innate self. Those of us who have advanced to the stage of passing on information will give freely of it to help the ones who wish to climb the ladder of learning.

I was led to the bottom rung of this ladder in a most circuitous way. Each happening was a step up, but I am aware that I have only made a start toward the ultimate heights. Nevertheless, I have the urge to stop at this point and project what I have gathered before I get too far away from the beginnings.

Five years ago, when the inspirational writing started for me, I was told it was from a son who had passed on at an early stage of his life. I couldn't believe it, until three different people at three separate classes gave me the same description of him. Then I decided this was more than just coincidence. Like a lot of others, I started with spiritualism in my search for new meanings to life and religion. It opened the door for me, and I must say contributed greatly to my progress.

Now that I've studied metaphysics (the philosophy of the real nature of our existence in the universe), I've thought often about that very touching encounter. Was it really a son, or a spirit guide, or was it my higher self who knew I required the personal touch in order to communicate? I have my convictions; perhaps you will too when you have finished reading this.

I am just an average housewife, mother, and ex-school teacher. Only by training have I been able to reach other minds to get the answers to the questions that all true thinkers have asked over the ages: Who was I? Who am I? Where will I go from here?

Follow through this with me, and you will see what one searcher found to be the truth. I can call it that with assurance, because I later discovered that others have also gained similar knowledge. Besides, I just feel it is good and right. This intuitional recognition is what we all should strive for, and this is the purpose of this book — to show how it can be done.

Perhaps you are dubious as to what is mental effort and what is divinely inspired. There is a fine line between — some can be proven and some can't — on either side. But belief can make you step over the line and become more fully satisfied and know greater spiritual joy. Who can deny this enraptured state to anyone? Once accepted, it will not let you go. You belong and are protected. You are at one with your creator. You and your God-given powers will never end.

It is hard for a college graduate to get down to a first grade level. I realize now how difficult it must have been for my more advanced teachers to reach me in the elementary phases of my development. The breakthrough has seemed frustratingly slow to me. But some have been kind enough to say that what I have attained doesn't always come in such a short time. I'm sure my persistence has helped. I have a relentless desire to learn.

Soon after I started classes, I was surprised to discover that I could see pictures of things connected with others in the group. Then, after a year of study, I began the writing from the source that had a semblance of unreality. But it appears that it is truly inspirational, because the words are often impressed upon my mind before they are inscribed.

There are three types of psychic writing, with these differences: completely automatic, as when the pencil is pushed even if the writer is reading or talking; partly automatic, when the writing is watched all the time or it ceases; and inspirational, when the word is imposed on the mind just before it is put down. But usually you do not know all of what is going to be written after it starts.

To accomplish this, the conscious mind must be held back by a steady concentration. But also relaxation must be achieved. This sounds like an impossible combination — to relax and yet to focus too. But it can be done by practicing the steps of the method of meditation, as outlined under "Guidance." Similarly incredible is the fact that in this state the intellect apparently is throttled down, but it is really put into a higher gear, and thoughts go at a faster speed.

But how do you prove whether what you obtain has a superior origin? (1) When there is a variation in your way of writing, such as words you don't normally use. (2) If opinions are different from your own, or if the facts are unknown to you and later verified. (3) If you are sometimes politely but firmly reprimanded. (4) If the contents are of a spiritual or intellectually-elevated nature. (5) Usually there is a tingling in the hand or arm. Sometimes there will be a tight feeling in the head. It is in the region of the temples when I have it. (6) There may be a slight tiredness at first, but it is followed by peace and contentment. (7) A fascinating thing is when my logical mind creeps in, once in a while, and presents a word similar to the one I've already received. Most often, the original choice is what is written down. This account was offered by one of my guides:

"Take the first word that comes to your mind, as that is our thought; the second is your conscious selection. That is what holds us up — when you try to choose — as this acts like a log jam in a river. The mind has to be confident. You know so many words that it is almost a hindrance, because you can always think of a better one; and then you wonder which was really our expression. If you can loosen up and not be so uncertain over who is doing the thinking, we can write faster."

It is said that it is simpler to use the psychic's own vocabulary than to try to get new phrases conveyed. Therefore, if the person is intelligent enough to have a well-stocked storehouse, the options are better. The only disadvantage, as has just been shown, is where there is too much to draw on, and this creates resistance to what is trying to be channeled.

Thoughts are sent through the magnetic atmosphere, and

15

the awareness of them can be instilled in the subconscious mind. After the reception of the idea, it is projected to that part of the brain that regulates the nerves in the fingers. The hand then does the writing.

This explains why some mistakes are made: Since we know that the transmission is made in magnetic surroundings, it is possible others have tuned in to the same station, so to speak. Consequently, it is easy to see how a message you think is accurate may prove to be mixed up with another's opinions.

The following paragraphs will give a summation of the channels who supervised my activities:

John, my son in spirit, was with me until March of 1972, when Mia Rama, a Master Teacher, announced that more energy was essential, so he would be my communicator. At this point, I was not as upset as I would have been earlier. I checked the dates and found that it was exactly two years before, that I had first been in touch with my son. I didn't want to give him up, but I realized that if I was to progress, I must let go and let God's more enlightened ones help me. In the earth life, we have to release our children so they can advance more. But in this case, my son would have to allow *me* to go on. I knew he was still with me however. And by now I'd had more time to get used to the association with Mia Rama, so I was not fearful of putting my trust in him.

A clairvoyant in one of my classes described him as a dark-skinned, gray-haired East Indian, who had a stern visage, but was patient and gentle. He needed patience to put up with my slowness! I could attest to the sternness too, because I'd been taken to task a few times, even though it was in a kindly way. For example, when I had to leave one town and go to another, because my husband Jay got a job there:

"The move will not help you to develop as well as you could here. But what is your desire — to please husband or self? To take a long time to reach your goal and have an inferior instruction? True, you can continue with this writing, and a book can be published. True, you could teach classes, but it would not be of the high caliber which you'd achieve in this city. But if you are willing to work industriously with us, we can help you attain your aims, though the quality may be less."

The final words that had the signature of Mia Rama were a bit terse, but I had smiled over them, because his disapproval had seemed so earthy: "When you stop asking questions we can begin the material you are to recount."

I wondered if he just gave up, or if I was ready for more uplifted souls. Evidently the latter was what was intended, because I had two more teachers: Chou Wen Lee and Theocrites. Here is an explanation of their mission as part of the Brotherhood of Master Teachers:

"We are called the Hierarchy, though we feel it is too pontifical a name. The simpler words appeal to us. We have regard for those who call on us for advice, because we need to help you as much as you require our aid. We progress according to how much we can guide the seekers.

"Our purpose is to establish a concerted, effective way to put forth our ideas to those of you who are receptive to them. Our thoughts are God-oriented and originate from the Universal Mind. The more involved aspects of our transmission are carefully monitored and directed to your superconscious. Especially the predictions and reincarnation material must be routed the way of this channel in order to assure accuracy.

"It is not essential that we declare we are Master Teachers or that our names be given. But in writing a book, it has a more definitive and personal approach when you can specify who your contacts are. This has nothing to do with ego on either side. True, you cannot determine for sure who is doing the communicating, but the material speaks for itself. Nothing inspired will come through a lowly soul. Your higher self learns to rule out the imposters.

"The higher degree of evolvement of our Brothers should not put you in awe of us. We were once within your range of achievement. And wise men do not forget their beginnings."

*A*fter our two sons had finished high school, I had more time to devote to my new-found study of ESP. I had taken a para-psychology course, and it was as if a door opened for me. I began to have precognitive dreams and clairvoyance. We were told to keep notebooks, listing and dating all our experiences. I've also kept letters and clippings to prove things that were acknowledged as evidential.

Finally, I went to Cassadaga, a small spiritualist community near us, and had readings from the mediums there. I went three times, and they revealed things they couldn't have known through the ordinary channels of perception. The last one told me she had a friend in St. Petersburg who had study groups. So I decided I'd like to live there where I could be close enough to learn more about this psychic development.

My husband was exhausted from the strain of his work on the Apollo project, and we'd talked about going to another place where he could semi-retire. Our vacation on the Gulf beaches proved to us that this was the location we wanted.

The first meeting I went to was one near me where there was an afternoon message session followed by a night class. I only went once, as I had a feeling of uncertainty about whether some of it was genuine. But one thing happened that was to change my life. A student medium next to me said that I had a son in spirit; that he had brown, wavy hair and was holding out his hands to me, but I didn't accept him, since I wasn't aware that he was in the spirit world. I went home and cried a bit over that. I had lost a baby twenty-one years ago, but I hadn't believed it could live on unless it was born alive. And there seemed to be much speculation as to when the soul entered, which might determine whether the infant continued to exist.

When I asked how to regard this situation, these very consoling words were given to me: "The fetus that departs before birth has been the attempt of a soul to belong to you. But for various reasons, mental and physical, the entity deems it advisable to leave the earthly plane. This lack of having a body in which it could dwell does not mean it was any the less desirous of being claimed as your child that might have been. It was just reaching out — a brief touch upon your heart. It is, and always will be, a son who really wanted to be yours. The entry of the soul is not a necessary requirement before you can say, 'This is my son in spirit, and I know that he will eternally be mine, though it could only be by his silent wish.' "

I found that the class I'd been told about in Cassadaga was quite far into the city and met in the evenings. I didn't like to drive at night. Neither did I care to sit in complete darkness, which was their procedure. Since I had a slight phobia along that line, I took the night light out of my bedroom and soon got over that obstacle. I noticed that I was about the only one who couldn't see lights or forms in the dark. This was most disconcerting, because I thought I had made pretty good progress so far. Seeing things in dreams, and all the carefully-logged experiences, meant little to this group. Nevertheless, I attended faithfully for three months.

I was privileged to get into a small class that had a very spiritually-minded teacher. I am sure that without her guidance I would never have achieved what I have. All those months I did not see a thing with my eyes open, but I soaked up the religious atmosphere like a blotter. We sang the old hymns I thought I had forgotten. Our lessons were provided by a Master Teacher who was communicating through a medium in the church. The discussions on these studies were interspersed with wit as well as wisdom. We laughed often, and it didn't detract a bit from our learning. Reverend Fulmer was always called by her first name, we had such informality. But she taught us well, and helped to interpret the symbolic pictures the students visualized for each other. For the second time, someone described my spirit son as having dark, wavy hair. My other two sons have light brown hair.

During this period, my visions and dreams increased, and I was able to hear and smell things with my inner senses. But the long trip and winter weather were finally too much for me, and after Christmas I regretfully gave up the class. A year later, the church was moved farther out of town, and I was able to study under Cora, who had been a student when I was. Being a natural psychic, she'd developed speedily and soon became a very elevated minister and teacher.

Meanwhile, I discovered that Reverend Green had meetings closer to me. She was a former school teacher and conducted her classes quite methodically. When we sat in the dark, we all touched hands and feet, so there was proof no one was moving around doing things — like raps, for instance. They were heard often on the wood-panelled walls. The room jutted out from the rest of the house, and the outside was concrete block. All this provided confirmation that no living person was involved. While I was taking her course, I began to hear taps in my small, windowless bathroom. But it wasn't until I did the writing that I found out who it was and how it was done.

We learned how to relax and meditate, and I had fairly good success with psychometry. We studied the Bible, and also the technical names and meanings for the various psychic categories. She gave commendable public readings, and my relatives were depicted in ways that were verifiable. But best of all was the message that told me my son in spirit was studying to try to help me. Little did I know then to what extent. A third different person also gave me the same description of this son. I was informed I should give him a name. I chose John, since it was a family name, and also one I liked. A woman told me how to do what was called automatic writing. A few days afterwards, I followed her advice, and this is what happened:

I sat blindfolded in the dark bathroom, with a pencil touching a pad of paper. All at once, the pencil began to push across the paper, making humps like a series of m's. This so astonished me that it was a second before I could think to ask who my contact was. From the movement of the strokes, I sensed that the name *John* had been transcribed. Then *I Love You* was pushed out in large, connected words.

I was so happy over this that I tried again the next night, which was the Saturday before Easter. I was dismayed when I found that the writing was undecipherable. As I looked at the letters under the lamp in my room, I wished that I could unscramble them. My pencil, which was on the paper, suddenly moved — there in the light, and with my being able to watch it!

I glanced at the clock. It was after midnight and Easter morning. What more wonderful evidence could there be of life existing after death?

It took me two hours to bring out two sentences; but they were meaningful. The first one was: "Your spirit boy not your only one." I suppose he used the word boy because he thought I expected him to be just a small child. By now I've read, and been told by him, that children grow up quickly to maturity on the other side.

The next words were certainly suitable for Easter morning: "We wouldn't suffer so much if you prayed more." This evidently had the broad scope of meaning that all of us should pray more for those in the spirit world.

At first, all I wanted was to get personal questions answered. John was very patient and put up with several pages of this. His script, which had been larger than mine, now became the same size, but was more rounded and easier to read. His remarks always made sense. All I had to do was cross t's, dot i's, and punctuate.

I was curious about how he was accomplishing this uncanny activity. I could see the muscles twitch in my hand; a finger would be pulled over, and the pencil shoved into a better position. Yet I was not conscious of doing any of it myself. So I had to ask, "How do you make my pencil move?"

"By motor movement through your mental brain."

This sounded a little obscure to me, so I looked up motor in the dictionary and found that it had to do with bodily movements, and motor nerves aroused muscles to action. From this I surmised that he could, by contact with my mind, cause the nerves to manipulate the muscles of my fingers to write.

Once I questioned if it was my thoughts that were emerging, as I could often tell what was coming next. But John stated that he helped give me the right answers, and the ideas were not originally mine.

One of his first declarations was a correct assumption of my feelings. "My words come slowly, but I guess you don't really care." Sometimes I got exasperated over the delays, but I was so happy that he could inspire me to write, that I truly did not care.

This statement further expressed our difficulty, but it was full of sadness and consideration and had no overtones of criticism:

"I'm so glad you found out about me, as I was lonely without my mother knowing that I lived. It is so nice that we can talk this way, by thought, as you can usually sense what I want to say. We do get stuck at times though, don't we? I can't always get the letters to flow from the pencil with ease. I'd better stop now, because your hand is hurting."

I had to shake my arm quite often to relieve the cramped condition of my hand and fingers. When I inquired as to how long we should write at one time, I discovered we were going over the allotted interval. His excuse was that I wrote slower than some; and I know that is true, as it still takes me longer than any others I've talked to on the subject. The only occasions on which it went with any rapidity were highly-inspired ones.

It was confirmed that I was to write a book; and after many months, there were some exchanges about whether I was ready for a Master Teacher yet. I couldn't imagine that I would be, at this early stage, and had no desire for anyone but my son to communicate with me. However, after several weeks of constant typing of the material I had accumulated, there was a loud rap on the wall. Since this was done only at special times, I sat down to determine the cause.

"I have this to tell you — a Master Teacher has been assigned to you. His name is . . . Rama." (I struggled with this, as I have poor recall on earthly appellations, and evidently it was also a weakness in my psi ability.) "You got four letters right. Maybe next time. . . . He wants you to try the breathing exercises before writing each day and at night too."

I finally got the name Mia Rama, which was declared to be correct. I had finished the typing and hoped this would be the end of my endeavors; but I should have known better. John declared, "There will be more to include, now that Mia Rama is with us. He wishes to tell you about his concepts."

When we'd first started, I inquired whether John could predict things for us. He intimated that he couldn't because he had not progressed enough. I suggested that people who read this might like to know how we can have fore-knowledge of events, and some examples of this ability. Rather resignedly, he admitted that it probably was an earthly desire, and he would ask for a more enlightened one to aid us. He re-minded me, though, that we couldn't always be right, due to the conflicting conditions, which have already been mentioned.

I received a vividly-descriptive account of how predictions are accomplished. He began with the statement that time there goes faster:

"That is why many can foretell the future; because it has already been seen happening here. This could be called 'parallel time,' but ours runs ahead of yours, and all episodes are acted out here first. It is like our making the movie, with you as the actors, but we see the preview before you get to see the show. You still have free will as to how you act it out, though."

These reflections were continued after I expressed my curiosity as to how sensitives can give such veritable replies to our questions.

"They reveal the answers as they see them on our 'movie screen' of your lives. What can't be disclosed hasn't been per-formed or decided yet. We go forward only so far as conditions can be foreseen; though some things are discerned farther in advance than others. This is due to some people casting longer shadows. In other words, they have a little more thrusting power to project their futures upon our life screens."

I considered this a most lucid account, and was proud of John for presenting it in such a simplified way.

This observation was added later by Mia Rama: "Time is the element that causes the most perplexity in our inter-world communications. That is because we have this more accelerated speed, and therefore we can see further than you can. However, this makes the results of predictions uncertain as to when they will take place. The reason is that we are out of touch with your time sequence; so we may say we perceive an event and expect it to happen as we view it, when really it is in your slower-to-come future.

"The important thing is that we understand the time barrier that is caused by your reduced rate of vibrations. Think of two trains running on different, but parallel, tracks. Then consider that one has a more powerful engine or fuel, which will naturally allow it to go faster.

"Because of God's presence, we are furnished with that extra stimulus that lets us proceed with more impetus. Thus, if you desire to come closer to our eternal world, get nearer to Him. He will give you more strength and wisdom."

I did some research, trying to understand more about time in our world, hoping it might shed a bit of light on its relation to time on the other side. I knew some good examples, but wasn't too sure about how to explain them. Looking up Einstein's theory of relativity only added to my confusion. Finally, though, I assembled my material; and these were my conclusions, along with a few definitions:

Time is an orderly proceeding of indefinite duration, calculated by something that exists, acts, or happens. If the world were a vacuum, there would be no time, as there would be nothing in it to move or cause time to pass.

Space is a continuous distance extending in all directions, and within which all things occur.

Some say the future can't be known because it hasn't happened yet. Then the present can't be real either, since it has gone by as soon as each specific event is finished. Yet we remember it. So why shouldn't the future have reality for us, if the past and present do?

This is one of the plainest ways I know of to illustrate how to view time: If you are riding down a road and there is a house ahead, that is the future. When you are beside it, that is the present. After you go by, it's in the past . . . but it is still there.

A similar situation is regarded in the comparison of different ways in which we travel: If walking, you see the road, the trees, and then the house. If riding, you note all of them, but at an excessive speed. In a plane, you observe it as a complete picture and even more swiftly. In the last example, it must be the relation of time and space that produces the composite image. This places the scene in the time-as-a-whole bracket . . . continuum.

On my first trip by airplane, I was astonished to notice that the waves on the beach were just still, white patches; and the cars didn't seem to be moving. How do we account for this? We can theorize that these things were at an apparent standstill because space and time are dependent on each other, and the viewing distance from the plane to the ground was in some way related to the airplane's velocity.

An illusionary impression is illustrated by imagining a ride in a car. From inside, it looks as though the scenery is passing rapidly by the window. But if you protrude yourself outside, you realize that the car is the object that is in motion. You have expanded the amount of space to be visualized, and you are aware that the type of movement is dependent on this.

To summarize: Our world presents a wider vision to the other dimension because they are at a more upraised stage of consciousness. Therefore, if we can learn to project ourselves into a more spatial spirituality, then we can envision a greater degree of the future and events related to it.

* * * *

Telepathy is the transference of conditions of consciousness between two people without using the ordinary senses. It is an exchange of ideas, or impressing the mind of another in ways which include touch, smell, seeing colors, pictures, feeling pain or other emotions. For instance, some sensitives have "taken on" the illnesses of others, though they were far away and the condition unknown. We usually think of it, however, as a thought exchange.

Some are of the opinion that telepathy may not be a forceful emanation, as we comprehend that energy depletes with distance. Space, though, is not recognized as having the same characteristics in the psychic world as in the physical.

Assume that the mind does not need space or existence in the physical body. If this is true, then it could go to the place where it could find the information it wants. This would apply to astral, clairvoyant, and dream travels.

Others believe the controller comes to the receiver and impresses him with the ideas to be offered. To spirits, distance is no barrier, so this can be considered as a source. Also, if both those in the flesh and in the spirit can communicate with their own kind by telepathy, then it follows that the living and the discarnate could share thoughts this way.

During a thunderstorm one day, I sat for meditation, and Chou Wen Lee, my Chinese Teacher, emphasized these opinions:

"It is more difficult to get through to you with this kind of weather, since it hampers transmission through the ether. Thoughts are received by electromagnetic waves, and as in the radio, it causes static or interference when two electrical energies meet.

"Distance is not a deterrent to us though. Only in the physical sense does energy become less, due to the dimensions of space. The mind can indeed extend itself beyond the limits of the human body and reach us here. By the same token, we can contact you, regardless of the remoteness. It is not necessary to say one way or the other is the only way it works, because both are possible."

Preceding the Apollo 13 launch, it had been forecast for me that there would be an explosion previous to the take-off, but no one to be injured. Instead, it took place when the astronauts were in space. Afterwards, reports said that it might well have happened on earth, since it was discovered that the oxygen tank was possibly damaged at the factory. It certainly was a near miss, and one that would have been envisioned by better eyes than mine.

Before the Skylab was put into orbit, I was assured that it would be successful. So I challenged this when problems arose. Chou replied: "We're not always able to see defects which may transpire. Some are more gifted here, as well as there, in foreseeing disasters. This does not mean our predictions on worldly affairs will not come true. It is just that some are not viewed as clearly as others in respect to the particular instant or type of an occurrence.

"The space workshop will be set back only momentarily because of this. The overall picture is one of success, as ways will be found to correct the problems. (And they were.)

"Wiser than we, are the mechanics of space vehicles. Our minds prefer to dwell on the spiritual, but we try to satisfy your desires for earthly knowledge."

No doubt they must feel very obstructed by our desire for everything to be absolutely evidential.

One of the most veritable messages conveyed by telepathy and inspirational writing was produced unexpectedly one day, when I was thinking of Louise, who had lost her husband three years before.

"Tell Louise that Dick sends her love, and that she will know this is from him by these words: The western trip was not good for you. Why did you try to think of ways to tell me you wanted to re-marry? I knew you did, through the telepathy we have, and it is alright with me. I don't know who or when it will be, but you have to be careful of some of those wolves. They might be after your money too. I will always love you, my little thrush."

When I first talked to her about this, she denied that her husband had ever called her that pet name. But later she admitted he had used the expression "my little bird." So he was just being more specific! The trip would not have been good for her, because she had a cold; and she was needed to take care of the children when her son's wife had a death in the family. On the re-marriage, he must have been referring to the times she asked for readings about it at meetings. She said the word "wolves" was one he would have used. This was indeed one I was able to prove all the way through.

It was June 4, 1970, when I saw something that seemed to relate to a well-known person. I was told at first that I should not include it in my examples of prophecy. However, on rechecking, I found it would be allowed if I did not specify who it was until the event came true. I had seen a picture of this religious personage in a magazine just a few minutes before I closed my eyes to rest them. I began to visualize a lot of red rosary beads; even the color in back of them was red. This image stayed with me so long that I felt it had special meaning; but I also realized it could have been association. I opened my eyes and then closed them again. This time a cross stood out very plainly.

I resolved to ask John about it. Briefly, he informed me, "Something will happen to this person within the year. This is all we can tell you. It is not to be revealed at present." On November 27, there was an attempt on the life of the Pope.

Besides reading Cayce's revelations of the southeast states going under water, I'd noted those of others who contended Florida would be inundated within the next ten years, which would be too little time to enjoy this lovely state. So I sought my son's perception about it.

"Florida will not be under water at the dates you have read, but may in the future, as Cayce said. Time is unknown yet, but there will be warning of it, and you will be told when you should leave. I can't tell you just where now, but can later when it is all seen more clearly."

Since my older son is in California, I was also concerned where he should go to escape the earthquakes so many have foretold. John indicated that Terry should go to the North, as it was less likely to be affected seriously than the South. This was given to me prior to the 1971 'quake in Los Angeles. And it surely wasn't my conviction that the best area would be in the northern part of the state.

This final paragraph was added: "We can keep natural disasters from affecting those we love, if they have enough belief in us and in God. This is done, not so much by averting the misfortune, as by advising you when and where to go. This is a service offered only to those who have the faith!"

* * * *

Intuition is a quick, instinctive impression of the truth without any conscious reasoning. In its lower aspect we speak of it as a hunch. In its higher state it is from the superconscious level and considered a keenness of insight. It may also be attained by way of telepathy, from those on earth or from the spirits.

I sensed danger once when we were going shopping. My eyes were closed to rest them from the glare of the sun. When I glanced up again, there was a street sign with the name Lookout. I had a sudden sureness that this was an indication to watch out for trouble. In the parking lot, we might have been hit by a car, if I had not been prompted to turn my head to see it and say, "Look out!"

When Tim was a small boy, we were walking by a canal, and he was swinging his jacket around. I opened my mouth to say, "Be careful; it may go into the water." And in it went, before I even had a chance to express the words.

Another time, he had taken his pet chicken out of its cage. I just happened to be by the window and noticed that he had left it alone while he came into the house. I called to him to go back quickly, as it could be killed. When I looked out again, a dog was carrying it away . . . dead.

Ellie, a friend from Texas who studies psi also, stopped to see me on her way up North. She asked me to write for her, but I didn't have the usual quiet because my husband was leaving for work, and her children were in and out of the room.

Slowly the words reeled out: "You are not intend. . .ing to stop at the nation's capitol."

Just as I was writing the word "intend," I was interrupted. I had sensed it was to be "intend. . .ed." Ellie said she had expected to go to D.C. With unusual certainty, I replied that I was sure it was meant that she would not stop at Washington.

A postcard from her disclosed that she had missed the capital city, "though a friend in Atlanta might have had me drop her there if she had come up with me."

I had a deep depression on Friday, January 22, 1971. It was like the sensation I'd had the day preceding my sister's funeral in the same month only two years before. I had received the notice of that from Eve, my friend from our home town. Now, this year, I knew from her late Christmas card that her husband was very ill. Had Kiley passed on? Was I now experiencing concern for her because she had shown it to me?

It wasn't until the next month that the note and clippings came, telling of the funeral service held for him on the twenty-second of January.

J have tried to classify all experiences under certain headings but there is bound to be an overlapping of types, since there might be a combination of the elements of clairvoyance, clairaudience, or telepathy. This does not even include the mention of precognition, which is the most evidential factor, because the event is seen beforehand, and this proves the psychic abilities of the senses. Therefore, I have picked the characteristic most predominant in each episode and placed it in the most suitable category. This chapter will deal mainly with the senses of smell, touch, and hearing. "Clear-seeing" is discussed in "Clairvoyance" and "Dreams."

The smelling of things not actually there is an uncommon occurrence. However, I had two or three that were most convincing. I was told that it could be done by projecting the idea to me, and then my physical senses would bring back the memory of it.

I was thinking of my grandmother, who used to come to St. Petersburg in the winters, and wishing I knew where she had stayed. Suddenly, the odor of medicine came to me: the kind she had inhaled through a cone. She used this when I was a young girl, and I had not recalled it since then. Nor can I bring it back now, by striving to recapture it.

The most wonderful things have happened at Christmas. Perhaps that is because it is my favorite time of the year, and the spirit of giving is in the air. I was sitting in our wing chair that resembled the favorite one of this same grandmother. Gradually, I began to realize that I was smelling dried rose leaves like the ones she had kept in a bowl. This also took place the next night, and I told my husband about it. A short time after this, I got a letter from his mother that was scented with roses. Then I was given a present of dried rose leaves in packets. Twice I smelled it physically, and twice received things physically.

There was a diminutive woman minister who sat by me at one class. She often wore violet-colored dresses. Several times I noticed what seemed to be old lavendar perfume. When others recognized it too, I asked if she used that scent. She said she didn't. Our teacher then commented that it emanated from her because of her deep spirituality. I am sure this was not due to our conscious association with the violet color, because sometimes the odor was not in evidence. So I must assume it was externalized to us in some way.

My earliest encounter with touch was when I was dreaming of my son Terry, and I felt a faint tap on my cheek. Strangely enough, I received a letter from him that morning.

It was certainly a helpful soul who woke me the day I had to get up early to wash. I dreamed of pulling sheets off the bed; then I was touched lightly on the mouth and forehead — a gentle rousing to duties to be done.

Other sleep disturbances were more annoying, such as when I was given a jab in the ribs or pinched. One morning I was having a bad dream and got poked in the shoulder. I even saw the finger pushing out at me just before I woke up from the "feel" of it. This was a compilation of things I didn't like very much. But, as John pointed out, it was my own fault.

"You left the door open by asking for recall of dreams, but not specifying for the meaningful ones only. Thus you were awakened to remember unpleasant ones. The punches are sometimes done by entities who like to play pranks on those who forget to close the psychic door by saying their preventive affirmations. You have built up a fine immunity, so don't let it be lost through neglect. The training you have received has been thorough and should be helpful to others."

This might be a good place to bring up the importance of study in a class for these reasons: There is the power drawn from the group and teacher which helps you to develop better. Then there is the guided step-by-step approach and the learning of affirmations as a precaution. One I say daily is: "The White Light of Truth surrounds me, protecting me from all negative thoughts or conditions."

Some of the bothersome things slipped in on me because I wasn't careful enough. I was able to correct all my troubles, since I had good guides advising me. But others might not be so lucky if they try it on their own. I was not warned about it at first, and this is why I have described my occasional ventures — to enlighten the few who might have to learn the hard way.

For months I had listened to those in our group speak of the psychic coldness, which I understood meant the presence of spirits. But I had never noticed it myself until one night when I was trying to give a message while we were doing psychometry. At that moment, I could feel a freezing numbness creep up my foot and leg. I wasn't frightened — just pleased that I had experienced something the others had.

I had the same satisfaction the only time I saw anything in the dark with my eyes open. When a woman mentioned seeing a lavender light, I looked in her direction, and there was a lovely mist that moved about in changing shapes. It came over by me, then vanished.

I wondered if anyone had touched me when I was at home, because I recalled having "cobwebby" feelings on my skin now and then. John gave me a good example of this while we were doing our writing one day. Something brushed my leg lightly. I rubbed it, thinking it was an insect. When it was done again, in the same place, I asked about it and was informed that Lassie, our dog who had died, was there with me.

This led me to question if animal spirits were always around on the other side. He replied, "No, they are in another area. This is to prevent the overrunning of them here. Those who have jobs to do, and can't watch over them properly, can see the pet when they are free to enjoy it. We think, also, that pets should be allowed to enter your world since they were your close companions in life." Animal lovers take note!

Marian was a newly-found friend who also did inspirational writing. One day when she was getting a message from her guide, Gray Eagle, she inquired if he could touch us, and he responded, "Absolutely!"

I requested that he do it for me, as I'd had it happen before and would know how it felt. When she asked where it would be done, he wrote, "Hand."

I sat many minutes with my palms down on the table, my eyes closed, breathing regularly and quietly expectant. All of a sudden, I noticed my thumb jerk. I opened my eyes, and saw that the finger was slowly extending out to the side. I called Marian's attention to it, and then it dropped back down.

It was odd to have this type of action, instead of just the light contact I was expecting. But we were told, "The thumb was made to move, as you were not anticipating that, and it was visible to Marian. A touch would not have been proof to her."

Once again it happened — in class while students were talking. I interrupted so they could see it. When the thumb was lowered, my fingers tingled, so I flexed them. The released energy

32

quickly went down my back and out at the base of the spine. It was momentarily painful, and I gasped. The teacher said it was due to spirit control, and that I should hold my hands up in a cupped position until it could dissipate gradually.

The next time Marian and I got together, two startling things took place. We placed our fingers on the table, closed our eyes, and briefly breathed deeply. Soon I felt as if I wanted to speak. I whispered this to Marian.

I could tell that the hair was rising on my arms, and my eyelids fluttered wildly. A mental conversation went on. An inner voice suggested that I calm down. I indicated I would accept a speaking engagement if I wasn't put too far out to get back! I must have been reassured about that, as I managed to relax completely. I opened my mouth slightly, not knowing what to expect. Phrases came into my mind. I sensed I was to say them, and I spoke haltingly:

"Guru with you. Our words will be . . . for you [two] only. Mia Rama says . . . you can do this . . . if you try. Marian can be . . . a medium. Will can heal. Together. . . ." Then it faded away. (Will was a family friend who did become a healer.)

I was weak with incredulity after this. But Marian wanted to go on with our experiments. She called on her Indian guide, and again he astounded me by an unexpected move. John's words, recorded the next day, describe the whole thing better than I could.

"The lifting of your arm was done by Gray Eagle through mind control. He had you feel a desire to have a push of the left arm. Then, to be sure you did not know what was to be moved, he had the right side manipulated by getting the idea quickly to your senses. Your wrist was raised, and after that, the hand lifted until your fingers completely left the table."

"The speaking you did was a form of semi-trance. A few words at a time were presented to you — like you get them from me, only you had the urge to speak. As was said, you could develop this. But it would take much effort, so writing might be your best mainstay

I doubt if either Marian or I have any wish to progress in this way; but we've been shown we have the capability.

After I asked for more facts as to how they can see us here, John said this was possible: "When the thought is followed by intense focusing, then the haze that is between us is penetrated, and you are visible to us. It may appear to be simple, but is really more difficult to do. As you know, the concentration you must achieve for this writing takes time and effort. So it is with us. And since we have so many duties here, we do not often pierce through that denseness.

. "The sound barrier is not as great as sight, though; for the reason that the atmosphere is easier to penetrate with auditory vibrations."

I'd been curious about this for a long time: "Can you hear everything we say here?"

"Only when we 'tune in,' and that is just once in a while when we think it is necessary to see how things are going, so we can guide you better. And you must mentally desire this to be."

Clairaudience is the technical name for the perceiving of sounds or voices without the use of the physical ears. I had a number of these which had the semblance of reality.

As I was waking up one morning, I was conscious that Jay had said "Hi" to me in his familiar, drawling way. I sat up at once, but he was in his usual, deep sleep. John accounted for it:

"This was done by likening Father's voice in your inner ears, and then making you aware of it."

One day I was in my room and was sure I heard the door-bell ring — just once. I got there promptly, but no one was in sight. A short time later, the same thing happened. I looked out to see a neighbor walking away from the door — after just one ring of the bell. Besides being clairaudience, it could have been telepathy. I had undoubtedly picked up the intended visit of the friend, who has psychic abilities herself. They say we are better attuned to those who have rapport with us in any way.

As I was drifting off to sleep one evening, I heard the hearty laugh of a friend from Ohio. About two weeks later, she and her husband unexpectedly made a weekend visit. This was another case of several types of ESP being evidenced. So were the following two examples:

Tim had been out all night after a graduation party, and I was thinking he should have returned. I was in the kitchen and had the impression the door had clicked, as it usually did before it was opened. But no one was there. As I stared at the door knob, the phone rang, and my son was calling to say he would be home soon.

One of the most beautiful of all the perceptions came about as I was driving into the city for our holiday party. All at once, ethereal organ music played the chimes of a familiar song. Then it faded away, and I knew for a certainty that it was no physical sound I had heard. I began to hum the tune and the few words that came to me: "Sing choirs of angels, sing in exultation. . . ." Strangely, I could not recall more of the verse, or even the title. When we sang the season's carols around the piano, I found it was from "Oh, Come All Ye Faithful." But why not the first part which I knew better? Christmas morning I had the answer, as I unwrapped a present of six little angels singing in a choir.

The Christmas we went to Virginia was full of happenings. I was able to answer unknown questions asked mentally by our niece. She was astonished, and wanted to know if I could read her mind. I had no idea what she was thinking, but evidently my spirit friends did, as I was told they helped me with it. There were also conversations with Jay's mother, who has seen and felt things too.

We had a bedroom on the first floor of the home of two other relatives. I had felt an awareness of the spirit of Allie's husband from the moment we entered the room which he had occupied in his last illness. That first night I awoke with a start at three — that seems to be the hour when I am disturbed if there is anything unusual going on. There was a sensation of eeriness, but nothing else until I started to drop off to sleep; then a whooshing noise in my ear startled me.

Two nights after that, at the same early morning hour, I was aroused by a loud thump, as if a heavy object had fallen onto the floor. Both of the women we were staying with had rooms above us. I was sure if something was wrong, the other one would hear it. In a minute, footsteps sounded on the stairs; there was a rapping on our door and a voice calling for Jay. For a heavy sleeper, his reaction was much quicker than mine, as he jumped up and was upstairs before I could get moving and follow with his robe.

It seemed that Allie had tried to get up, but got dizzy and fainted. Jay said he could feel no pulse, and she was cold at first. But she was warm when I was left with her while they called for the ambulance. I patted her head and quietly voiced a brief prayer. Two hours afterwards, she came back from the hospital walking and talking, and appeared to be just as well as before.

When we arrived home from the trip, I requested that John give me his account of it.

"The first three o'clock awakening at Allie's was done by us to give you a warning that something would transpire later on, and at the same hour. We could foresee her in trouble and wanted to prepare you for it. The swish of sound was an attempt to tell you what to expect, but the words did not reach you due to the lack of strong vibrations between us; the energy pattern was not built up enough. You had the opportunity to be helpful, and, perchance, to heal through prayer to God."

I can't quite believe I could have accomplished that; but it was an unusual recovery, considering the condition of her health, and the fact that she might have had a stroke.

CLAIRVOYANCE

Clairvoyance is the general term for the observation of things invisible to the normal eye. Inner impressions are gained without the aid of the outer senses.

Psychometry is using the sense of touch as a stimulus to induce pictorial facts concerning an object or its owner. This is possible, since all articles have absorbed the life record of what has taken place around them; and a receptive person can pick this up.

My method of doing it is to relax completely, close my eyes, and calm my mind. After the picture starts, I try to focus it in front of me, as one would do with a movie camera. If it stays with me long enough, then I know it is not just my fleeting imagination.

Here are some ways to learn how to do psychometry. Practice them in the order given and with the eyes closed: (1) Visualize a water lily on a pond. It is opening slowly on the lily pad. Notice all the surroundings: is there a bank nearby, frogs, fish, what colors? This may be done with any of nature's species. (2) Place your hand on the page of a book or magazine which has only pictures. Attempt to see in your mind's eye some of the colors or parts of the images. (3) Real objects given to you should have been worn only by the owner. And the background has to be known so you can check if what you see is evidential.

At first, symbols may be shown as the simplest way to get ideas through to you. But these have to be interpreted, and it can be difficult unless the meanings are understood. Some books have lists of these, but the subjects are endless and would be hard to memorize. It is better to rely on the impressions gained by the psychic or by the instincts of the one involved.

I finally mentally asked that I be allowed to envision actual objects related to the person's past or present, so the proof would be more substantial. This was granted, with the results that follow. I started with only seeing three or four things in an hour's sitting; then I progressed to as many as ten. There were only a few times when no acceptance was noted. These could have been something to come in the future.

There was one that fell into the class of moving from one article to another in order to clarify the intention. First, there was a cloth fastened loosely about the waist. Then it was pulled together into a cummerbund; and at the last resembled a corset. When I remarked that I had a notion there was a constriction in that region, the woman admitted that she'd had a hernia. I didn't know what a truss looked like, but my son had worn a cummerbund and my grandmothers had corsets.

Another three-in-one conglomerate revealed what it was, but not the exact significance. A train whistle, headlight, and chair car pertained to a relative who was with the railroad, and not to a trip, as might have been expected.

For a woman I had just met, I observed a warship with something going off the side — like depth charges or torpedoes. Her husband had been on a destroyer during the war.

There was a question to ask about this one: Would a sea-horse be draped over the arm of a chair? A man claimed he'd lost a tie-pin of that design, and it might have been in a chair.

Sometimes things seen are most convincing simply because they are so unrelated to the person. For a blustery, ex-Navy man, I had a glimpse of a grand piano. I discovered that he had a relative who had a baby grand; she had also performed on a large one. Butterflies for this person also didn't seem plausible. But he recounted how he had enjoyed them lighting on his fingers when he was a child on the farm. It made absolutely no sense to me, but two pipes and a black cross turned out to be stretcher handles and the symbol on a rescue truck, both of which had been used in his work.

A knife held for a friend conveyed to me a house that looked as though it had been burned at one end. I was told it was true that there had been a fire in one room at the end of the house, caused by one of the cigarettes this person smoked almost incessantly.

I don't often get names, as they can't be presented visually. However, Olga was imprinted on my mind, and I also discerned an hour glass. The teacher confirmed that this woman had come to her for advice which she didn't follow up on for some time. Oddest of all, I met Olga a week later. Because of the uncommon name and her psychic interests, I asked if she was the one described to me. She was reluctant to admit that advice was received, but did say she had visited Cora.

One other name led to no matching picture. Since it was for the teacher, she suggested that I work on it and see what else I could get. White robes on hangers were disclosed, along with a stained-glass window. I stated that it must be someone connected with her church. Then Cora told me that her son, whose name I had spoken, was a choir boy and wore white robes.

Precognition hasn't entered into this field too much for me yet. But the sitting with Ellie, the friend from Texas, produced a surprising turn in that direction. As I held a piece of her jewelry, a waterfall appeared. She had been to Niagara Falls but had no plans to go there on her trip north. However, after she left us, I was the recipient of a postcard from there that said, "How's this for a waterfall? You certainly were psychic with my bracelet!"

Sometimes people don't use their intuition in trying to recall adequately places where they've been or things they've seen. Houses on a hill seemed unpainted or stained to me. This was not accepted by a man who had traveled in the service. I mentioned that pictures of homes in Alaska looked like that, but he hadn't been there. My husband indicated that Switzerland's were similar. When I related this to the man at the next meeting, he acknowledged that he had stayed there, and the houses did resemble my description.

When I started to view something for a student, a cold chill went over my arms, and my hands and feet tingled. I asked if someone had passed on, because I also noted a brief likeness of a death's head. She said no one recently. It occurred to me to inquire if anyone was seriously ill. Then she conceded that her brother had just had an operation, that tubes had been put into his feet, and that he hadn't been expected to live. No wonder my feet had a prickly feeling!

In the very first class I went to, the teacher handed out a pin, which I discovered afterwards belonged to an ancestor living years ago. I visualized an old stone fireplace with no fire in it. There were also some ruffled curtains near it. Then my eyes shifted to a staircase that curved at the bottom, and there were indistinct figures ascending it. It was confirmed that the relative had a house with the interior just as I had described it.

Wanderings are what I call the ones where you go back into the past of people and survey one thing after another associated with them. The first time this happened to me, it was as if I were walking through the woman's old family house. I couldn't believe

I was really observing every item so correctly. There was the turn of the stairway, the stained glass window, table, lamp, curtains, and so on.

I have never been overseas, yet I viewed many different things in Germany and Bavaria where Sophia, a student in our class, had lived. These included a church with many spires, where she was married; steps up to a castle, and a big, carved door with a shield design on it; the dragon's mouth of a statue; a curved bridge over a river and a domed turret, which she said alluded to her Russian heritage.

I sat around the pool with a new acquaintance, wrapped a towel around my head, and proceeded to amble through her life, glimpsing an interesting diversity of subjects that started with an underground cellar, a hand water pump, wash bowl and pitcher, a goat, flowers by a wire fence, and ending up with a diamond and a condominium she hoped to buy. It really showed how she had come up in the world, and was a great character study.

When I received these words for Celia, I was most unsure of the reaction I'd get if I repeated them: "Monkey see, monkey do." But my friend laughed and declared that she often chided her pets with that remark. I also glimpsed an owl for her and found out it was her favorite bird, because of the "wise old owl" expression. Subsequently, I discovered that she had been a Phi Beta Kappa in college.

For some reason, I have great rapport with beauty-shop operators. I had been able to discuss ESP with one operator in particular, and while I was drowsing under the hair dryer, I had a vision that was not precisely correct; and yet the beautician could claim the happening. There were bunk beds of dark wood, and as I looked, the top mattress seemed to fall down. She immediately remarked that her brother had fallen out of the upper berth on a train. The wood was always a dark mahogany, as I recall. An odd tie-in was that our Tim fell from his top bunk as a child . . . . Worth noting here is the fact that we are shown things that we've known or had occur; that way it is easier to get the idea across to us. It is evidently presumed that the contact and contactee will have enough intelligence to put two and two together. Several times I've seen the old brass bed my folks had, and when I'd present it to my friends, they would agree that there was one in their family also.

I couldn't understand how I could have insight of things for people when only first names were known, or in some cases, none at all. This was the explanation:

"Through a record file we have on everyone, we can instantly detect facts about any for whom you seek information. Names are not needed, because a sensor picks up your concentrated thought on that person, and also the picture of him, or her, as on a television set. You see, we have our computer systems here, too!

"The data is then transmitted back to you — by impression on your mind of a picture (if clairvoyance is the method being used), or through the projection of words, if you are writing.

"Think of it as a simple telephone call to headquarters requesting truths from the Heavenly Bureau of Information — our version of your F.B.I.!"

At church one morning, I tuned in to some strangers and distinctly saw a tree tapped for syrup. My curiosity had to be satisfied, so, after the service, I turned and asked if it related to them in any way. They smilingly admitted that it was a product of Pennsylvania, where they lived. I didn't even know this, thinking maple syrup came only from the New England states, where I had visited.

Intriguing clairvoyance came from my teacher to me. Cora envisioned a man in a bakery using a long paddle to pull out the bread. I spoke up, saying that my husband had done this briefly years ago. She added that he should put on a mit when he put his hand in the oven, as he might get burned. When I got home and told Jay, I found it had already happened to him the day before. This was unusual postcognition, with no telepathy possible through me.

Cora warned me at the end of a class that I should be careful or I would get myself fenced in on three sides with only one way out. On the way home, I was in the right lane when I spotted a patrol car at the intersection ahead. Unwittingly, I pulled over into the middle lane, but ended up face-to-face with the police car which had parked in front of me. Those to the right wouldn't let me over, and there I sat for at least five minutes. Finally a car allowed me to get into the outside flow of traffic, and I was able to move on. The left lane would have been worse to get out of and not the way I wanted to go. So I certainly was fenced in — and less than an hour after being told about it. It was a minor accident, and it is doubtful that it could have taken place at the time she perceived it.

Paula and her husband wanted to sell their motel and get a house. I tried to get something on this. When I saw gold on the sand and an oil well going up into the sky, we all laughed about it, as it sounded so preposterously prosperous. But later that month, an oil spill floated up on their beach. Eventually they sold the motel and have a good income from it.

Several visions appeared at prayer time. I hoped that indicated they were more inspired. Two that came true certainly were, though I wasn't sure what they meant at the time.

One began with my seeing a house on a hill with snow on the roof. Next I noticed the sloping roof of a bedroom like the one at Lowell's. Since I knew of two homes that fitted the outside description, the inside room needed to be shown so I would be sure who was involved.

The evaluation of this was brief: "Write Mrs. Lowell now, as there will be trouble connected with the house before the snow comes."

It was not until her usual Christmas card that I received an answer to my letter. It was unbelievable all that had happened. One grandson had died; another had a near-fatal brain concussion and operation, and her son had a heart attack. To top it all off, the water pipes broke in the house, and it took two months to replace walls, ceilings and pipes.

Just after midnight of February 9, 1971, I visualized a town in a valley. As I looked up at the hill above it, the sides began to crumble away, like a landslide. Then I was viewing a railroad trestle; but I didn't understand why.

At six that morning, there was an earthquake in California, near where my son was located. I was told that they were trying to show me the scene of a 'quake, but I saw it in a milder form. The trestle was to make me think of Terry. I had assumed he was with the railroad, because he had said he wanted to work and travel before finishing college. Also, his girl's father was an executive with the Santa Fe Railroad.

When a letter finally came, we found out he wasn't working then and was still in school. But I thought he was, so this symbol was projected to me for identification purposes. However, in the summer and fall, he did work for that railroad. This would seem to have been a sort of latent precognition.

As an exercise in a book I was studying, I once attempted

to travel clairvoyantly out west to Terry. I could easily picture the states as I passed over them, since I had made the trip before. But his apartment was unknown to me. The time was 10:30 p.m. I observed him seated at a desk with a lamp that appeared to be the gooseneck type. The color green was around him, as if on the walls.

In his letter replying to this, he commented: "Near coincidences make your mental visit rather interesting. On that date, at about 7:30 p.m. our time, the niece of the landlady delivered some green curtains to my room. Before she came, I was seated with my back to the desk listening to records. The lamp is not the type you saw, but I own one like that — my girl is using it."

The green curtains were there, soon to be hanging up on the walls. He was at the desk, though in a different position. The time was the same, allowing for the three-hour difference. And he had a lamp like the one I imagined. There were four things so nearly right that it seems more than mere chance. The only way I can explain this when one is awake, is that there must be an extension of perception — that somehow the subconscious personality can act independently.

One year, Terry had left us after a Thanksgiving visit, and I was concerned about where he would go for Christmas, because he had said he didn't want to stay with friends or the only relative he had in California. As I was thinking about this, I had a clear glimpse of steep, dirt hills and the top of a pine tree. Still, I just couldn't believe it when I found he had spent that holiday camping in the mountains, surrounded by coyotes!

A friend of ours had died very suddenly. His mother, Mrs. Norris, wrote movingly of a vision she had of her son. I'm sure she won't mind if I quote it in part:

"There are times when I feel I can't stand it, not seeing Kip . . . At first I was very upset and prayed a good deal to know if he was happy. Then one Sunday after communion, I was back at my seat, and Kip came to me — as real as if he had been standing right in front of me. It was just his face, with a cloud around him, and it was all in color. He smiled and nodded; then he was gone. But now I knew he was happy where he was. . . ."

This was a wonderful experience, one that I envy, as I have never been able to see anyone in spirit like that. I can testify that she is not one who would hallucinate. She does a great deal of church work and is engaged in many other worthwhile activities.

This was remarkable proof that we live on and can come back and give our loved ones a sight they will never forget.

*T*here are two main sources of dreams: The subconscious — yours or the collective thoughts of others that you may contact. The superconscious — which gives spiritual help and advice pertaining to our lives, and all episodes relating to ESP. This higher faculty travels out to meet a superior awareness, and in sleep, this is naturally at work in everyone. The inner senses are never at rest.

The classifications are: (1) Physical — caused by feelings concerning daily problems or adjustments necessary for the body. (2) Emotional — relief given from mental repressions. (3) Spiritual — inspirational guidance.

Things to look for in a dream: It may be warning you about mistakes being made; presenting solutions to a problem; disclosing things overlooked about self or others; and communicating with those on the higher planes, which can be most beneficial.

Meditation helps clarify dreams and relaxes the hindrance of the conscious mind. If you aren't able to find time to reflect, then you may be reached by the way of dreams that rouse you to the comprehension needed.

When I asked John if our guides assist us with our dreams, I got a short dissertation on the subject: "We can project our ideas, but the mind must be made receptive, so it can see what is desired by the sender. This is done by injecting the thought that we want admitted to the intellect and getting its acceptance. Then we present the picture. If there is rejection at any time by the dreamer, he is able to wake up. Recalling usually depends on the fact that you just had the visualization a few minutes before, and that you requested the channels to be open to reveal it."

Once I had a dream that I must have refused to approve, because I awoke suddenly. When I searched for the reason, I received this comment: "That unpleasant one was the result of overwork. The mind was too stimulated, and your imagination reacted with abnormal results."

Later on, I was getting so many dreams that I objected, because I was being wakened up earlier than usual. He said this was necessary, since I had such an active mind, even when asleep; and he had trouble getting the images to me before I woke up.

"We can't break in on a dream you're having, as a telephone operator could interrupt a call, but have to wait for a time when your 'line' isn't busy. And that isn't often with you."

"Why do we have dreams that appear so real sometimes, and yet there is no truth to them?" I asked.

"This is because you have thought about the people or events at a time in the past, and the ideas get scrambled by your subconscious, which has too many things to keep track of. It is hard to distinguish between the realistic and the unrealistic, but ask for guidance in seeking what is true."

However, I took advantage of John's more lofty nature to help me decipher my images now. He usually had logical explanations, and between us we managed to figure them out.

A strange one was made clear to me after I'd read about traveling in space. He made this prefacing statement: "You can visit our world with your other self, but you do not like the idea of extensive astral travel. Accordingly, we come and meet you at the places where you would want to be."

In this case, I was apparently at our family home back in Iowa. I ran to close the doors, because I knew someone was trying to come in. When I got to the back, I felt an unseen presence already there. A chill passed over me, and I awoke with the same sensation. My sister Grace, who had died the year before, was the one who wae with me. John said, "She wanted you to see the house again, since you both loved it so much. But you were frightened and tried to shut the doors, which caused you to wake up."

Many months after this, I finally had an astral flight in my sleep. At first it seemed to be levitation, as I was doubled up and scudding along about a foot off the ground while others walked beside me. Then someone lifted me up above the buildings. I expressed my dislike over being up so high, and was lowered to the street again. A tap on the glass door made me come to and remember it. But no one was around, so I infer it was a psychic activity.

In another instance, I was floating around just above the ground. I commented that it was easy once you made up your mind you could do it. Then I saw my grandmother, and asked if I had washed the dishes. When she responded that I hadn't, I knew I must return and do them. Just the idea of this uninteresting task brought me back to consciousness. John remarked that this was real astral travel recalled. "You were met at the old home to get you used to flight at lower levels so you will not be afraid to come to our dimension, where you can see all of us and exchange thoughts. You have been here, but recollecting is difficult for you, as your mind still resists it."

One morning I awoke so dizzy that I almost fell over. I was not too surprised at John's response to my inquiry. "You were not well balanced after you returned from here in your sleep. You noticed a jerk and a swirling sensation as you came to wakefulness. That was the astral body re-entering. Next time, maybe you can remember the visit with us." So far I have not been able to do this, much to my regret.

My husband was going to see our younger son across the state. The day he left, I had a dream in which a car was about to go over a hill, but stopped at the top. There was a steep drop below, but there were steps leading down. My writing indicated Jay might have to pull off the road because of an accident ahead, due to a car coming from the side road. The steps showed there would be a way out of the dilemma. When Jay arrived home and reported that there was no such happening, I was relieved, but also disappointed that we were wrong.

However, just two weeks later, he saw a crash of two cars caused by one coming out of a side road. This was the scene described to me; but he didn't have to stop, as he was across the road ... a way out of the dilemma. The time discrepancy followed the by-now expected pattern of partial accuracy.

There was one concerning Tim that led to my calling every hour for twelve hours, trying to reach him and find out what had happened. I've had many intuitive incidents connected with him because he is so outgoing, and I worry more about him. I couldn't bring back to mind the visual part of the dream, since I didn't write it down, but someone was whispering two names to me. In my attempt to hear them clearly, I cupped my hand to my ear, and this movement woke me up.

I had John write down what he knew about it. He saw that fraternity brothers were with Tim in the car. There was also a girl and a patrol car in the picture.

When at last I contacted Tim on the phone, he acknowledged that a week before, he had been parking in the car with his girl when a patrolman pulled up to check on them. But it wasn't until weeks later, when he came over to visit us, that he admitted the fact that in the last month he had played football and was hit on the head. This caused a slight concussion. Fraternity brothers realized he wasn't being coherent and took him (in the car) to a doctor.

These two separate events, until put together, seemed like an uncompleted jigsaw puzzle. As for the names, they were spelled out by John as Rentsen and Hoffstater, and this was how they had sounded to me. I discovered that two people named Benson and Hoffricter were students associated with Tim's fraternity. The last named was from the same town as a deceased relative on my mother's side. Isn't it odd that out of all the boys in the house, one from my cousin's home town was chosen?

Around Thanksgiving, I viewed Tim as being at our former neighbor's home for a meal. Mrs. Wellman called out to tell me to come over. I went to the house, but a brown dog, penned up inside, snarled at me, and this caused my quick arousal. Tim came to see us that day. He admitted he had been to eat at Mrs. Wellman's exactly a week ago. Also, she had found a new, brown dog to replace the old one that had died. The actions of the animal symbolized the anxiety I must have felt from our son's thoughts, because he told us he was leaving college and going into the service.

After the first hurricane of the season had started up the coast, I had this visualization: two large, gray rocket shapes were going low overhead with a loud, droning sound. I could see them come down into the ground to the north and east of me, but there was no flame. As usual, I consulted my helpful one.

"This means that the storm will come in near you, but not close enough to make you have to leave. We used an image that would attract your attention by its intensity. Be thankful you have us as a back-up weather advisory!" The storm turned into a tropical depression and went to the northeast of us.

Just prior to our taking a short trip, I saw myself on a road that went up over a hill. When I put on the brakes, they felt squishy. I didn't think to relate this to my husband, simply because I was so busy getting ready. But after he had the car checked over, he mentioned that the station attendant discovered the brake system needed more fluid. This certainly shows that we all should heed the advice that is imparted while we sleep. Some may say they never are shown anything of significance. But if you will open your mind to the possibilities, and pray for this kind of guidance, it may be given to you.

It must have been precognition, and no doubt telepathy, in the one about Polly, who is unusually psychic. She was surrounded by young people; mostly girls' faces appeared to me. I wanted to talk to her about something, but she said she was too busy. Four days later, I got a letter which was dated the day of my dream. In it she stated that the teaching she did at the school kept her absorbed and "busy." When I saw her a month later, she confirmed that her group now was of both girls and boys, but eventually she would have "mostly girls."

I'm not likely to forget this spine-tingling nightmare: I saw a man running; he was getting smaller, and had a horrified look on his face. Someone said, "He's getting away — stick a pin in him!" I know now that this meant I was trying to go too far too fast. Just the past night I had begun an experiment in the back of a new book without going over the lessons leading up to it. Something black swooped over me and blotted out what I was trying to see. I turned over though, and went to sleep. But then I woke up in the middle of the night and couldn't doze off again for several hours. When this occurred two more nights in a row, I was really upset, and had that creepy feeling that is brought on by fear of the unknown. I called my teacher, and she assured me that it was probably one of my guides protecting me from attempting something that was too advanced for me. She told me to try to see the God-light surrounding me before I slept; and after that I had no more trouble.

Probably one of the most amazing dreams I've had so far was about a high school friend named Kay. I was behind a glass window and called out to her twice, but she didn't hear me. She appeared to be getting a ticket, because she gave her name to someone in a booth, and people were standing in line behind her.

I had to write two friends to find out her address, and when I at last received a letter back from her, it was two months to the day that I had the vision. She remarked: "From May 12 (the date of the dream) until my aunt died on May 27, I was upset, wondering if I might have to go to California or to Iowa." (Her aunt was dying in the West and would be buried in the Midwest.) She went on to say that friends in both places took over for her, so she did not have to buy a ticket. But her worry about it reached me, even though I hadn't corresponded with her in over twenty-five years! Further proof of the person who probably helped out in California was given in a letter from my cousin, in which she wrote that a Mrs. W. "took a great deal of responsibility" for Kay's aunt.

This same relative also explained two other dreams I had. One was about her brother, and the other concerned two friends. All were my age, and we were in school together. These premonitions might have come to me by thought transference, because she said, "I am interested in your powers of perception and clairvoyance. My husband has ESP, and we have been fascinated with this. It surely is a science, and one which should not be taken lightly."

I had seen her brother as he was when we were younger. I was passing by and asked cheerfully how he was. He answered, "Not so well." His sister revealed that he had been ill for several years with a disease that deteriorated the brain, and now he was quite child-like.

It was unusual that I had the second perception the same morning. Mrs. Parnell was a friend of my mother's and had twin sons. I spoke to her and inquired about them. All she said was, "Only one." Then I saw the faces of two boys who looked alike, but one of them had lost a leg. The other had a knitted turtle, and I got the idea he made them to sell.

Cousin Dory wrote that the one son was "in bad shape — failing with cancer." He lived with his mother. The other resided in the same town and undoubtedly was aiding his brother, as the turtle signifies strength and resistance. Over a year later, I was notified of the death of the twin. Now there was truly "only one."

To affirm the results of something I'd seen the year before, I'll quote from a letter of Terry's: "I went camping in Mexico with a group of college students. While there, I fulfilled one of your dreams that you had, Mom, when I was home. Remember the one about me running into trouble near the pilings? You thought that might mean the pier I was swimming to every day. Well, the pilings turned out to be those of a bridge that crossed a stream on the beach where we were camping. We went swimming near the bridge, and got caught in the current and outgoing low tide. We had to overcome both the offshore currents and the cold water, plus going back through the breakers . . . . We all made it out, but not without being scratched and cut on the rocks. Last week I just happened to relate your dream to this incident. Looks like you may have had a premonition!"

A precognition about Eisenhower was perceived about a year ahead of its culmination. It was May 2, 1968. He was smiling and running through a field of high grass. He seemed so young and happy, and I'm sure now it was a prevision of his soon-to-be-released spirit enjoying a romp in the meadows near his home in Kansas. Four days before, he'd had the first of four heart attacks that were to cause his death eleven months later on March 28, 1969. Early in March, he seemed much worse, and I didn't think he could live until May. But I was still certain the date of my dream was of some consequence. After his death, there were five days of tribute ending in burial in Kansas on April 2, 1969 — eleven months to the day that I had the dream about him.

Postcognition in symbolic form, and in both a vision and a dream, was the experience I had in association with my half-sister's death. I didn't know she had died at St. Mary's Hospital and had been buried on a Saturday in January, 1969. News of this was sent to me from my friend Eve in a letter which arrived exactly a week after Grace's funeral. The night before the letter came, I had tried to meditate and asked for something meaningful to come through for me. In a few minutes I envisaged a group of white-robed nuns walking toward me. Then suddenly their garments turned black. The next morning I was awakened by a frightening scene of rough ocean waves, which some say is a sign of death. But besides that, I had painted a picture of waves dashing on rocks for Grace, because she said they expressed so well the turbulence in her life. It is apparent that nuns appeared because she had passed on in a Catholic hospital; and the change to black robes certainly depicted death. I also recall that depression the day prior to her burial; a fact that stayed with me due to the synchronicity with the funeral of Eve's husband in January, 1971.

The most wonderful dream of my life was one which I shall never be able to describe adequately. There were two young men with me who appeared to be my sons. Another youth with dark hair leaned over to kiss me. The feeling I had was of deep emotion surging over me and then away, like the strength of an ocean wave; only it was full of love and beauty and goodness. As I woke up slowly, savoring the rapture of it, I knew I had experienced something that was far from this earthly domain.

Let me give my spirit's view of it: "This depicted your

desire to have your two living sons near you. But the kiss was given by me — to show you the pure joy of love from our side of life. It transcends that on earth with an ecstasy that is incomprehensible except to those who have been allowed to be aware of it, as you were this morning. This was revealed to you on account of the way you wrote about the love you feel emanating from our world, and your wishing to join us."

THE OTHER DIMENSION

J just could not believe that the descriptions of the spirit world were correct. At the beginning, I had only an excerpt from a book to go by, but John insisted it was exactly as given.

"Yes, we do have grass, flowers, trees, water and buildings. Our dwellings are not as enclosed or high as yours, but they are beautifully constructed."

"Can you tell us what is the substance you use to make these things?" I asked, "or would it be too technical for us to comprehend?"

"It is too much to try to make you understand this at present; so it is best left unanswered. The Master Teacher says it was discerning of you to have thought of it though. I am pleased to have such a smart mother."

I must add that I was happy about that too. I went on with my questions: "To us, here on earth, it seems as if you are so far away up there in that void the spacemen float around in. Are you really that distant?"

"No, we are nearer than that. The earth thrusts up into our world." (I had a time getting the word "thrusts" as it wasn't one I would have expected.) "The mountain tops are very near to us. So you see, we are not so far from you."

This rather stunned me, but I had to know more. "Is that why so many people had spiritual experiences when they went to the mountains?"

John replied in the affirmative, and began to quote Scriptural references about Jesus, Moses, and the prophets.

But despite all this Biblical assurance, I felt I needed a teacher's opinion as to whether what I was getting was genuine. The minister seemed to think we were doing all right, and would get better. I came away with the feeling that I should go on with it, and that the few suggestions made were more helpful than critical.

Later on, when I inquired as to what and where heaven was, I was provided with a more detailed description: "Happiness is heaven, you say, and since we know the former is a condition of consciousness, then you can realize that the unseen world is similar.

"We are near you, round about you, but apart from your material existence, even though ours interpenetrates yours. We are not in your world except when we wish to be — or you ask for us. Those who believe we are with you all the time are engaging in wishful thinking. We would not want to inhabit your rushing-around, car-and-plane-oriented reality. It is not our desire — or idea of heaven.

"Try to imagine that there are around you regional levels known as planes. These are believed to be real, flat sections dividing one area from another. But they are really invisible, vibrational barriers between each location of the upper realms. You rise from one to another as you evolve, and each has more beauty and enjoyment. Originally you go to a plane where there are those who have interests comparable to yours. Ones from the same countries usually group together also. But there is a universal language, so that is no limitation."

One question I asked John started several paragraphs of his observations. "Just what do you do for new arrivals?"

"We meet them and show them where to go. Those who have come here suddenly from accidents, war, suicide, or long illnesses, may be put to sleep for a while until they can accept their new state of being. There is usually someone with them when they wake up. They need to be comforted and told what to expect in this different world.

"The new souls are given a thin, white covering, like a robe, to put on. Relatives and friends gather to greet them. After this, they are shown where they can take studies they would prefer, or how they can help others to progress.

"Many have to learn how to think telepathically. This is more difficult for those who were not very good at thinking things through thoroughly before; but all advance according to their ability. Travel is by mentally concentrating on the destination and then directing yourself to it.

"When we take them to see the beautiful things here, that are so much like the place they just came from, they feel better and adjust with more ease.

"We have houses to live in; we don't just float around in space, you know. We can be together with our families if we wish. Your father has built a replica of your old home, and you may reside in it, or create your own.

"When you come here, you don't have to be with marriage partners with whom you were not congenial. Anyone you don't want to see will be kept from you by your own restrictive mental powers."

According to his next remark, there is not supposed to be any ill will where he is located, though the lower spheres must have an abundance of it.

"We do not have feelings of revenge or resentment. These are earthly characteristics that are too inconsiderate to be allowed. No one can tell me that vengeance is a satisfying thing. It is like hate, and that erodes like acid. It is a continuous disease that can be cured only by acquiring more spiritual knowledge. But many would rather have hate than make the effort to overcome it."

One day I let him talk on his own and this came out: "There is an incredible radiance of light over everything on our plane. It is unlike your sun in that it is not so hot. It gives warmth to us at all times, but it is a uniform glow that is regulated by the higher spheres. There is no night.

"Only the lower regions have darkness and coldness. The people's dwellings there are hovels compared to ours, which are built as we wish to see them. They are in this area because they had committed crimes, or omitted living in harmony with the laws of nature. These include matters that would appear to be trifling to some — such as cruelty to people when they should have been uplifted, or persistently indulging in evil thoughts.

"Hell could be considered as the name for the mental anguish and judging by the soul itself, as it reviews what must be reaped from that which it sowed. There is no fiery pit, but the soul is separated from people or things that are greatly desired. And it must remain in the lowly state until it can overcome all the wrongs by forgiveness and purification. Then the entity can rise to more pleasant planes.

"Knowing about all these things will make it easier for you to adapt when you come here. I wish this could be soon, so we could talk together and see each other. But you have many more useful years of life there yet. I will be here whenever you want to contact me. When you arrive in this dimension, we will have no more communication problems. Then I shall be able to show you the true way a son can love his mother — by kind deeds and acts of devotion."

There are moments such as these when I desire to join that heavenly crowd. The more I find out about the after-life, the more I look forward to going there. There is a love that far surpasses the earthly kind. I wish I could trade places with one who dreads to leave here because of fear of the unknown. I can only hope that this writing will make more people realize what love and beauty await them in the other realm.

I think mothers, who have been deprived of a child by its passing, would like to know the answers to the question I posed to John as to why he couldn't stay here on earth.

"I could not have a good body. My chromosomes were not well developed, and I would have been lame."

Nothing in my old medical book confirmed that any of this might be possible. Then I found an article that reported a case where a baby's cells contained an abnormal chromosome. The infant had deformities of the foot and hips, among other things, and it died. Sometimes I feel that I am guided to reading these facts that seem to be essential to convince me — and others.

John said that anyone who passed over with a physical deformity lost it completely on the other side. There were mothers, too, who took care of small ones as long as was necessary. Also, a baby living entirely in the spirit world had a better chance to evolve more fully: "I entered here the wiser because I had no physical wants to have to overcome. Likewise, the spiritual study was easier, as I had no earthly habits to unlearn."

At one stage of my studies, I became aware that I was needing more rest. When I asked Chou Wen Lee about this, I was surprised by his revelation.

"This is due to more being taken from you at night in service here. You do not recall, as it is done during deepest sleep. You record the entrance of new arrivals to the place where elevated souls are inducted. They require little rest, and so are sent on to the particular area where they are best suited.

"The work itself is not tiring, but the effort of the astral body to come to this higher level is a new and thus tiresome experience. We need more helpers, and can use those on earth who are willing to give aid. They have only to ask to do so in their prayers."

There is much more that could be written about in this chapter, but whole books have covered the subject, so I'll end with this quote from my Teacher.

"The subject of the after-life is feared by many on your planet, simply because there have always been taboos and doubts concerning anything connected with what happens after death. Then how do we convince them? It must be done by telling the truths as perceived by the ones who have been able to transmit them back to your sphere. The fact that so many of these accounts tally with each other is a sizeable proof.

"But it takes more than this to overcome the established opinions of some persons. There may be the actual experience of a spiritual phenomenon — such as the woman who saw her deceased son's face appear to her at church. It is truly remarkable to witness the belief and happiness that sweeps over one who has observed and accepted such a verity.

"The most distressing thing is that the unbelievers are diminishing their chances for easier adjustment when they pass over. And they are not lessening the fear of death which they now have.

"There is a hazy idea in the minds of some as to whether or not they are or will be immortal. By these words we can give them the assurance that they are:

"There is an inner body we cannot see, which is a duplicate of the one we use in life. When physical being ceases, this spiritual part of us passes on to a higher consciousness. With it goes our memory, and all phases of our personality as it was just evidenced on earth. In other words, we do carry on as before, but in a different dimension. Our mind recalls all that was done on the earth plane, and it can also add to the knowledge that was acquired there.

"The love of those left behind is still felt, and so is their grief. For this reason, emotions should be controlled, and only prayerful thoughts projected to the departed. Release all sorrow to the Father, Who will comfort you. But know your loved ones continue on — as did the Christ — and all shall meet again . . . with joy and remembering."

J had not even heard about this subject before I started psychic study and found that a lot of people believed in it. I disliked the whole idea of having to return and live another life, so I was more interested in arguments against it; and I had quite a few.

I preferred to stay with the family I had this time. I did not want to have a new set of relatives. I understood that I could come back to re-live with them again, but they would be different personalities, and not the same ones who'd been so dear to me now.

If there were no conscious recall, then we couldn't learn from our former experiences, and this seemed a waste of efforts to advance. I'd read that you can stay in heaven and progress, though more slowly. It appeared to me that in a spiritual atmosphere one should develop better. There were so many ways to help others there, and you could ascertain things to benefit those left on earth too — as my son was doing for me. Of course, persons who liked living in the physical world probably would prefer to think they had another chance.

In regard to giving reasons for musical geniuses, for example, perhaps they were inspired by great musicians on the other side. Why not give them some credit? There were numerous accounts of how they tried to implant their ideas in our minds. If we were more receptive to this, there might be a greater number who could accomplish remarkable things.

As to the feeling of having been in another place before, it could be due to stored memories, astral travel, or a dream that later was seen in actuality.

Then why did I decide to write about this? There was a build-up of unanswered questions. Why did John say that one of the causes for his departing was due to the problems involved; and why did he say he chose to leave? This sounded like a theory of rebirth that I had heard mentioned.

After a year of writing and reading, I made up my mind to ask for the real truth of the matter. I had no idea it would take several pages and days to complete the subject. I even started out with light pressure on the pencil because I was so sure there wouldn't be much to say about it.

I don't recall what my question was, but this was his answer: "I can tell you if you wish to know; but it will take time to do it fully enough to suit you. Yes, it is a true doctrine, but I have tried to keep from relating it because you did not like the idea.

"I thought it best not to stay on the earth plane, since I found I would not develop spiritually enough, and could help you more from here. But it took a long time to get you to make the contact! I tried to be born to you, as you had qualities I wanted in a mother. But I would have been lame, and that would just have added to your troubles.

"Terry's soul knew the conditions facing him, but preferred to take the chances in order to have the cultural background you could give. Rewards of it will be seen in his work.

"It is a fact that we are guided by a guardian angel to choose our parents, according to our karmic obligations to them, or theirs to us. But we also have free will to change the pattern, to some degree, if the situation does not seem suitable for the type of progress we require. Not all can be seen ahead, owing to changes of circumstances.

"Now to the history of your other lifetimes. You had harmed another, so you had to know what it was like in this life to be wronged. The good childhood was to give you a chance to choose the right way, but you were not prepared for the evils of the world and didn't have the strength to overcome them. This was partly the fault of over-protective parents, but also partly weakness of character which needed rebuilding into what you have now achieved.

"You had no recall as a child, but in adolescence you were aware of a strong pull to the past; as if you didn't belong in your particular era. This manifested itself especially as an intenseness toward English activities. The predilection to art on both sides of the family was why you were guided to that environment. Your lack of desire to continue with the talent was the result of being thrust into teaching it, which you did not want to do. This was on account of the consequences of a life in England, when you lived in Nottingham. As a child you were intrigued with the stories of Robin Hood and his adventures around that town.

The date of this incarnation was about 1600, at the time of

the Tudors. You were a tutor of English and very good at it. But you were an unmarried woman and too attractive to the opposite sex. You did not comport yourself as a teacher should, so you were imprisoned. This elucidates your dislike of teaching now, and furthermore, your fear of enclosure in small places.

"Tim was your father in a Maryland life, and therefore resented your present authority. He was a farmer named Nathanial Thurston, who died in 1838. You were his daughter, and did not like farm life, nor his dictatorial ways.

"The art ability was best when you were in Egypt and did sculpture, like the head of Nefertiti, which you have always admired. The vision of water up to your head was a disclosure of the way you drowned in a flood of the Nile, inside a temple by a painted column. You were a child of Father's then, and a physical mistreatment of him at that time had to be worked out now, when you were the one to suffer." (This last was given in detail, and it was a very clear revelation of causes and effects.)

"This all ties in with your life, you are thinking; but is it your invention? No, it is in the Akashic Records, although we know it is not provable until you come here. But then, this is only of cursory interest to you, isn't it? However, I think you will admit there is much that is veritable."

I must concede that every sentence has meaning and accounts for feelings I've had and things that have happened. If this were all made up by my mind, then I should take up short story writing as a profession! However, knowing that I have always tried to adhere to telling the truth, I am convinced that there ought to be fundamental explanations for it all. Before I explore these though, let me go on to some other examples.

I had a life-reading from Olive, a woman who could see the Akashic Record . . . which is an etheric substance whereupon there is imposed every thought, sound, and sight of anything emanated since the universe began. This enables clairvoyants to discern the past that is far removed from the ordinary senses. Strangely enough, she hit on many things I could relate to myself now. I'll repeat it just as she gave it to me, because of the unusual way in which it was expressed, and then I'll comment on the likenesses.

"We find the entity a relative of Queen Nefertiti and a tutor of her children. It was customary for the kin to live on the royal grounds. The name was Neverta. She was able to reprimand the children only in a gentle way, as no corporal punishment was allowed by the queen."

I used the paddle on my own children in this lifetime, and it was obviously an outlet of frustrations built up in the past — and present — as a teacher. An instructor in my parapsychology class told of visualizing me on a balcony of an Egyptian building, looking out at the sand and palm trees, and then turning to go toward the structure, which seemed to have an opulent setting. This was a welcome bit of confirmation from an outsider; nor could she have obtained it by telepathy, as the reading was not recorded until a year later . . . . There would appear to be a discrepancy here, since my writing indicated that I was a sculptor and did work, like the head of Nefertiti. But that could have been in another return to Egypt. I evidently was also a tutor in England. We repeat vocations and locations in various incarnations. Notice the repetition of art in each of the countries that follow.

"About 4,000 years B.C. the entity lived on a small island off Japan called Habuti. It was a remnant of a much older civilization, and flourished around 1,000 years before it was destroyed by earthquakes and volcanic action. These people had a religion similar to Buddhism, and they also worshiped the sun. Their skin was yellowish-brown. The women wore much ornate jewelry. They were graceful in movement and of fine bone structure."

I have always admired Japanese art. Also, I have a Japanese-American daughter-in-law. Perhaps we were together in that era so long ago. When I was young, I read about the volcanic eruption in *The Last Days of Pompeii,* and was quite frightened by it. I still am . . about earthquakes, too . . . which is one thing that has kept me from residing in California, as another place besides Florida, where I could really worship the sun.

"The entity was a carver of stone in an area around Rome. Made markers for graves, especially for infants. Designed rosettes and scrolls. Also made florettes of papyrus and wax. Dyes were made from earth colors, such as clay, and some from the willow bark soaked overnight. Entity should work with interior decorating."

This last would have been an ideal vocation for me, but it didn't turn out that way. Scrolls and rosettes are favorite designs I've used. In addition, I had remarked that my logical choice of a country where I'd do sculpture would be Rome rather than Egypt, as the latter's figures were so stiff and unnatural.

"On the African continent around 3,000 B.C., the entity designed jewelry: delicate rings and bracelets with small figures hanging from them, and made of bones and ivory. There was a belief in the protective ability of charms. A stringed instrument was played. Death was from a spider bite. This was regarded as an honor, and was supposed to guarantee a good after-life. It was considered a favor of the gods if there was a horrible death, like this one of gradual smothering. Some people put on an extra act of writhing and moaning for the benefit of those around them; but not so with this entity, called Kuta Kuta."

I can state emphatically that I don't care for bugs of any kind and have been known to become vociferous when I see them. But I don't believe in faking any ills or emotions. As for smothering, I've had this unpleasant sensation in the form of asthma; and I recently read that allergic people may have died in past times by suffocation. Of all the musical sounds, the strings are the least of my favorites. It seems likely that this could be the result of the tragic ending of my African life cycle, just as drowning in Egypt probably caused my present negativity to Egyptian art. We collect bones and teeth of animals, and have ivory objects from Alaska and India. I seldom go anywhere without putting on jewelry.

"Entity once belonged to a desert tribe in Arabia, and was a diviner who could find food and water through psychic powers. Name was Concenta. Created clothes and was held in high esteem."

It is a bit odd that the only time I was told I had psychic ability was by divining, because I had a pendulum when I first started my psi endeavors, and in one year I got ninety right answers to questions I put to it. As to all the art references, Olive had only met me briefly before the reading, and she affirms that she had no idea I had been an artist by profession.

Some time after this, I found I was able to attain a short past-life writing for those who requested it. I would not do it for anyone who did not have a belief in and knowledge of reincarnation. This way there should be no shock over the revelation, as they would expect that some unpleasant karmic situation might arise. It certainly did for Ruth, but luckily, she never inquired about it. I'm sharing it here because it has such an uncanny fitness to the troubles bothering her. She wanted to know why she was so alone all her life; why she had lost so much money in unwise ways; what she had come this time to learn; and why she couldn't sleep.

In class meditation, I had clairvoyantly seen many things she could claim in this incarnation. When I recognized a lion and a red cross on a shield, I was sure it had a connection to Richard the Lion-Hearted, and told her I would find out what it meant during my writing. Never could I have guessed, or been able to make up, the resulting observation:

"The entity was with King Richard as a mendicant (begging friar) during the Crusades. The life was one of hardship and deprivation. The number of men the friar killed must be compensated for; and Ruth came back to repay for all the lonely women left as widows from these slayings. The fatherless children were a reason she had none in the present." (I later discovered she had only an adopted son.)

"The friar, though a religious person, in those days often resorted to killing in order to get money or food to eat. The stealing from the rich, when he couldn't beg and receive it, is why Ruth now has lost so much from unscrupulous persons. This cannot be prevented unless there is more submission to God's ways in relation to all people with whom she comes in contact. She should be more charitable towards others, and think less of material wants and more of what can be given spiritually of self to others. This is what she came to learn. Then she can sleep."

Our minister was having problems with her daughter and suggested that I try a writing on it. Through psychometry, I had pictured a woman hanging from a board, along with other things indicating a Roman existence. Reverend Moore disclosed that she was aware that she had once been crucified in Rome. This is what was recounted to me:

"The young girl has a karma that is due to her mother's extremely religious nature. Her past life causes some of this, as she was a spiritually inclined one in the time that the mother was hanged on the cross. She recognized her mother and was afraid to make it known, much as Peter denied he knew the Christ.

"So she has this subconsious guilt feeling today; rejects spiritual things and has forbidden herself to be as close to her mother as she would really like to be."

Both of these are excellent evaluations of relationships, and far beyond any knowledge I could have had. It is possible to see how I could reach into my own storehouse for my life reading but to apprehend the past for others, it would have to be channeled from higher sources. Or maybe my consciousness tuned into the stored memories in the other person's mind, as Cayce said he did. He also claimed he had seen the records, though. When I challenged my source as to the validity, I was informed:

"The reincarnation readings are protected, because we are enveloped in a shield of God's Light for this to be funneled right to you . . . a necessity, since not just anyone is to be allowed to see the Akashic Records. This is your way to help mankind."

In case you may wonder how the unfolding of some former cruelties helps anyone, consider that to completely know and understand ourselves is the only way we can truly be of aid to others. Having insight of our past faults or affiliations, and benefiting by them, is learning, not stagnating. By facing what our purpose is in life and trying to improve ourselves, we gain stature. We are not the seed that falls on barren ground. The more we grow, the more we can give out.

Celia had an interesting revelation of me as a wife of the king's counselor at the time of Louis XVI, during the French Revolution. My husband's name was given as Bartellé. I was a governess for the queen's children, and also wrote stories for them.

There are many things here that piece together with this period of my life. I took French lessons when I was in grade school, and also began to write short stories then. I recall clearly the reading of *A Tale of Two Cities* by Charles Dickens, and the terrors of life at that time in history. And isn't it strange how often I was a teacher of some kind? This has come through three different sources. Likewise, on several occasions, I was associated with royalty. I'm glad I wasn't advised that I was on the throne myself, as I'm always suspicious of such egotistical claims. At least, my activities were reported by others besides myself.

There were some special references to my previous spiritual recurrences. They were from Theocrites, one referring generally to what my psi friend Jane had seen: that I was in a nun's habit and tortured by a rope about the neck. (No wonder I have so much trouble breathing!) Incidentally, Jane does not believe in reincarnation, yet, like Cayce, she gives it out when she channels. I went to Catholic school for a year, and once felt drawn to become a sister, but could not work it out then. This was my Teacher's expression:

"You were a nun twice before; thus, fortunately, we can draw on those past qualities from you. The next incarnation will be enlightened and easy for you, so do not fret about it. You will have almost all of the old karma paid off and be striving for spiritual progress only."

That was encouraging news if I had to return .... The other disclosure was made after an upsetting day and an ensuing dream that was interpreted in a way my conscious mind would never have admitted. As stated earlier, I thought it was presumptuous to acknowledge that I could achieve an elevated status, or that any higher souls would have an interest in me. Therefore, what followed was more startling and unexpected.

When I was asleep, a voice spoke softly to me, and I could feel an arm around my shoulder. I said I couldn't hear; and then I woke up, surprised, but not frightened by the touch. I recorded in my dream book that I had the notion someone was trying to comfort me. I sat at the desk to write, but I didn't get far.

"The touch was true ethereal contact from ...." Here my pencil stopped, and the words wouldn't come to me. I felt I was resisting, and I endeavored to heighten my consciousness. Finally there was movement once more. . . . "the Christ. He was attempting to counsel you. But the words were not heard, as you do not yet realize such a Higher One can be concerned over you, despite our many assurances that He is with you.

"You were in Rome in the days after His crucifixion, and participated in the activities of the Apostle Paul, learning as much as you could about the Lord and His wondrous ways. This is told you now to show you how close you were to His followers, and the deep spirituality you once had, which makes it easier for us to find and use the Biblical words in your storehouse of memories.

"So accept this Divine Presence into your awareness, knowing that you truly belonged to His worshipers then . . . and can today. Open your heart; release your soul to His words and deeds."

After this beatific experience, one more comment was recorded. It started off as if he was presenting a lesson:

"Now to the subject of receiving rewards for the good you do in this lifetime. The more you build up, the higher the attainment; and the greater your chances to come back as a more evolved soul. In this incarnation you were paying off an old, old karmic debt from Egyptian times. The fact that you put it off for so long shows how your soul realized the enormity of the debt. Also, physical features of some discomfort have been accepted, not to mention the renewing of your spiritual faith, which was sadly neglected in several past lives.

"So you see, you are accomplishing much now, slow though it has seemed, and painful too. But God will reward you as befits your deeds."

We are told that our pattern of life and the general outcome on earth is known before we enter the physical. It makes me shudder to think of the qualms I must have had in previewing my existence-to-be. But if I was able to foresee the improvements I would make, it must have helped.

The main question that plagued me, though, was why we weren't allowed to remember our mistakes of another era so we could rectify them without the misery of trial and error. In my subsequent reading, I found a few reasons which appeared to have merit: (1) In trying to correct a fault, we might dwell too much on that one thing and not give equal attention to other problems. (2) Realizing we didn't conquer a bygone wrong-doing might result in being unsuccessful again, due to over-anxiety. (3) Knowledge of all our past virtues would swell our egos and give no incentive to improve. Likewise, knowing all the bad could make us despair of ever correcting it. . . . So only what would be of the most benefit in the present situation should be manifested. We are qualified to uncover these facts when we have reached the point of perceiving how to contend with them. This is gained by suitable spiritual meditation.

One consoling thing to dwell on is that we may not have to re-appear again for maybe a hundred years, and by then things we haven't liked in this world will have changed. There has been much prophecy concerning peace after the year 2,000.

Reincarnation explains why we are attracted at once to certain people and dislike others; why we prefer special areas to visit or live in; and why we have certain phobias or fancies.

Children are closer to the records of their previous lives and quite often spontaneously erupt with recalls that cannot be explained in any normal way. If a child is a genius in a family of many youngsters, and if heredity is claimed as the cause of his talent, then why can't parents have *several* gifted children? Development of skill has to be ruled out, because most often geniuses have come from poorly-educated families.

Reflect on these random thoughts: If you have troubles, consider that you were probably given the will power to surmount them. . . . It is assuring to know that if you now have a proficient mind, you must have diligently tackled life's former mental challenges. . . . You may have to learn to be a good musician again, but the music will be of a better quality than previously. . . . Those who were handicapped by accident will be recompensed, because it was not their fault. . . . If you make fun of another's disability, you may have it yourself some day. The same with another race — you might have to come back as one of them, if you revile them now. . . . If there is a relative you don't have any rapport with, it could be that you planned the association in order to learn from it. . . . Make the most of your talents and time, so you won't be chalking up a sin of omission.

Rebirth is said to be a necessity so we can fulfill the law of evolution and become perfect through the ventures of living in the school of life. When we think how little time is spent by the average man on his spiritual improvement, isn't it apparent that we need more than one lifetime to reach the perfection God expects us to accomplish? Can you give yourself entirely over to His will, feel your heart and soul always at one with Him? Can you attain the level of an apostle or a master? This should be your goal.

When we no longer cause suffering, then our earth lives can be ended. Karma incurred in this life can be resolved now if enough effort is made. This is the law of compensation. So it seems that some of us can be given another chance. Are you trying to upraise yourself in every possible way, or do you wish to be reborn? Do you want to meet the same types of people and problems that you have now? Do you desire to go through the throes of birth, adolescence, old age, sickness, and death again? I don't, and I am doing my utmost to climb as far up that ladder of life as I can. I won't take the risk . . . there is too much indication that there *is* such a thing as reincarnation.

I was taking a course from a teacher who was channeling messages from spacecraft. I hadn't paid much attention to this because I thought it was literally too far out. All I was interested in was the meditation time. So imagine my surprise when I got my own communication, and it was as far out as I could go — planet-wise.

On the morning of November 28, 1972, I woke up impressed with these words: "Keep watch at Ethan Barber's sand knoll."

This made no sense to me, but it was strong enough to arouse my curiosity, so I sat down to write. It didn't start out with the usual signing in of Mia Rama, but I doubtfully let it continue.

"I am Za-Rena from the planet Pluto. The intention of our transmission to you was to tell religious light-watchers that a sighting can be made at the point now known as Nixon's home. It was called by the other name in past years."

When I tried to find out what year and place, I had my customary trouble of getting "up tight" and then uncertain of what I received. Since the President had two homes, I had to determine if it was the one in Florida or California. I'm still not sure which; and I've been unable to obtain any confirmation of whether anything was seen around the first week of January — the period that was specified. I would really like to know, too, if there was ever a place called Ethan Barber's and where it was.

After this message, my teacher gave me some booklets on space channelings, and I discovered most of the names were hyphenated, with the second one capitalized — just like Za-Rena's.

When I requested more information later in the month, I was given a reasonable explanation, but not one that satisfied my skeptical mind.

"Believe we were sighted, but cannot guarantee it will be reported to you. Even if the right people were alerted, our spaceship, *Plutodinus,* may not have been seen by them, since Nixon's home was difficult for us to locate. It was more isolated when we were here before."

The next reception from this source was quite unexpected; it was done very fast, and I hardly had time to know what words were coming next.

I had just read of a new way to meditate by staring at a candle placed near the forehead. I lit one, stared for about a minute, then closed my eyes. I had to do this three times before I could visualize the red flame that was supposed to appear. Then I had the urge to find some paper to write on. I was seeing images with my eyes shut, so I groped in the desk drawer and pulled out a notepad that I later discovered had been used by Terry, for whom I was trying to get something evidential.

"Your son was a man of Atlantis. He is to be a God-appointed Peace Corps worker, and will be helpful to many poor people. He is on the right track now. . . ."

It was indicated that he did not feel the need to finish college to do this work. Subsequently, Terry disclosed that he had been thinking of leaving at the time of my writing. But counselors suggested his chances would be better if he continued; and he did go on to graduate.

Further comments came out at another date: "I am of the light regions, and wholly authorized to contact you. You are protected by your affirmations, so do not be concerned.

"Since you accept the validity of UFO's, you are aware that we can hover over your earth, and therefore we can reach you through mind impression. My spacecraft is now near South Carolina, but distance does not hamper thought, as you know.

"Pluto may be farther away, but it takes us merely months to arrive here, not years, as would be required by your spaceships. Some day you will learn our methods. We have impressed on the minds of your scientists the present knowledge they have. When they are ready to progress more, we will impart our formulas to them. Our power is not like any you have thought of yet.

"We are not strange creatures, though some lesser-developed planets have primitive forms. These are not to be named, as research then would be rejected by you, and exploration is needed to increase your knowledge of the universe. There can be no harm in this."

The last paragraph was an answer to my questioning as to whether there were any odd-looking beings on some of the planetary bodies. I had heard of this, but it seems that it will be one more uncertainty we'll have until more is known. As to the coldness of the planet Pluto, it could have been warmer millions of years ago, and those who dwell there could have adjusted to the change, which was probably gradual.

Za-Rena brought out these ideas related to the above: "We do not live much of the time on Pluto, since it is so cold. Mostly we roam about in the mother spaceship, where we study and plan our excursions that bring us near you earth people, with whom we can communicate.

"We are not seven-foot giants. We are nearly five feet tall, and our faces more closely resemble the Japanese."

In a book I was reading, one section spoke of space entities having a very unusual height with light hair and skin. After I received my description, I found one at the end of the book which stated that there were some about five feet, with slanted eyes and tanned skins. From this, I guess we should conclude that they vary on different planets, as much as earthlings do in each country.

In March, these observations were expressed: "Our goal is to make earthmen aware that we come in peace and that we wish harm to no one. In our studies we learn about the topography of all the planets, how to read the Akashic Records and the Bible, as recounted in our language. We are part of God's Universe, too.

"All thought is universal, and your mind can translate what I want to say. Yes, we speak in a different language. But even if we met face to face, I would be able to project my thoughts so you could deduce what I wished to express to you.

"We have superior technical facts because we were once Atlanteans and came back to other planets, owing to yours not having progressed sufficiently for us. You and your son were in Atlantis together. He was a builder of many important structures; thus his interest now in architecture. But it is a passing one, since he is to work with people who are needy in this life. You are to teach the New Age."

This last was surprising to me as I hadn't been told previously that I was on Atlantis. And I certainly had no inclinations to do any more teaching. It was strange, though, how Terry went so often on hiking trips to Mexico. I was told that he migrated to that area after the flooding of the continent. We two were separated, and I went to the valley of the Nile, where I apparently resided at many other times, also.

All of these communications ended with the drawing of a

triangle. This is a symbol of the energy which the pyramid is said to generate. UFO's have exceptional power. Since it has been presumed that some on Atlantis escaped to Egypt, if they also went to Mexico and South America, that would explain why pyramids have been found constructed in those regions also. I never have had the conviction that those large stones were put into place solely by slave labor. If it was achieved by the skills the Atlanteans were said to have possessed, then these structures are more believable.

By summer, I was no longer getting writings from Za-Rena, and it wasn't too unexpected when I was advised that the source had been authentic, but not useful now. I can only suppose that this was just another encounter to produce for me a touching of all the elements of our evolution.

The Devil's Triangle

J had read about it in the newspaper, and decided to ask if there was any accounting for so many ships and planes disappearing in that area. This was my second try at it, since the first time I threw it away . . . not believing the Navy "Avenger" bomber contact.

I recall that one of the flight crew had the name that he reported so concisely: "Gallivan here. I want to tell our story again. This is the truth that no one else has tried to get from those of us who live on, to tell it — from the other side.

"There was a vehicle that rose up out of the water, causing it to churn white, like we broadcast at the last. There was no time to tell of the huge, round object that approached us, as our power was cut off. Then they used a ray of light like the laser beam, and completely eliminated all traces of our planes.

"Since being here, I have discovered that they do this to keep their undersea habitat a secret. And all who get too close, or who they know have seen them, may be destroyed. They are from the part of Atlantis that was near Bimini. They live under water, as we are learning to do, but are more advanced, and want no interference."

In a description someone gave of Atlantean spaceships, they

were said to fly and also go under the water. This could indicate the type of craft that intercepted the five Navy planes in 1945.

I recall a documentary film on the subject, in which a sailor declared he had seen an odd-shaped object descend into the ocean. Yet no one seems to have come up with any answers. Are we unable to discover more about these unknowns, or is it merely a case of not caring sufficiently? Whatever our reasons may be, there is no doubt the submergible inhabitants are not ready to share their secrets with us yet.

After all this was transcribed, I ran across something which dealt chiefly with these enigmas. In many cases it was stated that no debris was found afterwards. This goes along with Gallivan's disclosure that everything was destroyed — which a laser beam could do, according to what I know about it. He had said their power was cut off. Several instances were given where planes lost radio contact or had similar problems in the Bermuda Triangle area. The most significant factor is that more ships and planes have vanished in this particular location in an excessive proportion to those which have similarly disappeared in the *rest* of the world.

Perhaps we should presume that there are intelligent beings from other planets — or within ours. Owing to the frequency of sightings. it appears logical that they could be hidden in, and operate from, the water. There are plenty of solid mountains on the bottom of the ocean where they could exist.

Also, we are just beginning to explore the under-the-surface regions, which constitute well over one half of our world. So if others have been there for a long time, wouldn't it be natural for them to take action to protect their dwellings? These are only theories, but they could explain the phenomena.

Raps and More Raps

The raps on my wall had been a puzzle to me. The teacher had said that it was undoubtedly my son in spirit, and I chose to believe this was possible, because who but a faithful family member would always be there when I was?

But the method by which it was done was still unknown to me. Finally, I'd asked so many questions about it that the teacher took part of our class time to explain it. She likened it to the blowing up and popping of a sack, as if an extra energy were gathered up and then released. If it were powerful and rapid enough, then it could be projected into space and cause percussive sounds.

When I discovered from our writings that John was the instigator, I requested his depiction and he responded with two sentences that appeared to be logical: "It is accomplished by our being able to build up strength from your force field of magnetic, electrical energy. The louder ones you hear are from more concentrated efforts."

I have not had physics, and I had to do some research to try to understand the meaning of these words. Electromagnetic waves are extended (transmitted) through space or matter by exposure to the oscillations (variations) of a force field. These incoming waves are converted into sound, light, and other forms of energy. This is how we get our radio and television reception as well as telepathy, raps, and other psychic phenomena. Notice John said "your" force field, so we can conclude that we have our own built-in source of power.

Rap was really not a suitable word, as it was more like a tap made by the flick of a finger on the surface. At least that is how it was done for me, never loud enough to disturb, but able to be heard by anyone.

I had supposed John was with me in some spirit form when this was going on. But he said this was not necessary because he could do it by the concentration of his mind on the place to be tapped and then causing it to happen.

I was curious as to why the time between the raps varied from one-minute to five-minute intervals. This took some discussion back and forth, which condensed down to the fact that it depended on the conditions being right and regulating them, and this influenced the spacing of the vibrations.

Twice I called my husband to the door to hear it, and he left shaking his head, because he had looked all over and found no physical way for it to be activated in our upstairs apartment.

On several different occasions, I noticed a louder, popping noise that reverberated on the empty tub instead of the wall.

Once was when I returned from the class where I was told how this was done. Another was after a four-day trip, and I considered it was his way of welcoming me back. One night, following a day in which doubts had piled up, there was just one resounding ping again. I had to find out about this.

"It required extra force. I wanted to show you that we can do things unbelievable, so you will believe!"

Since I'd been told to try to see the God-Light, when I said my prayers, this was easier to induce by closing my eyes and lifting my head to the bathroom light because it was so bright. Then the taps would be heard on the side wall rather than the back, where they usually were. Upon my questioning, he explained that he did this because it was nearer the light, and thus I would note the "celestial" difference between the two raps. Most convincing are these illustrations that a source outside my conscious self is with me. "Spiritual" is the word I would have chosen, not celestial. And I recollect that it took a while to get it recorded, inasmuch as it didn't occur to me that he would use that not-so-common but no-less-correct word.

My friend Marian wanted to hear the taps, so we sat in the little room for about five minutes, during which we both were aware of them. Now I had two people to prove I was not the only one who was "hearing things."

Before we went on our vacation, I was informed that there would be no raps where we were going. For such a short time, the changes needed would require too much effort in getting the range of the wave length regulated and re-adjusting the distance the sound must go.

After two years, we moved closer in to the city, and many anxious days went by while I heard nothing in the bathroom but noise from overhead. The apartment was a lower one and not sound-proof. It was so disturbing, in fact, that I decided to say my prayers in the bedroom.

Evidently John also thought he couldn't compete with the movements upstairs, as I soon began to get my taps on the window by the desk in the living room, where I was writing. They occurred even when others were in the room, and at times when I was not near the desk.

The following was a startling incident, but was not repeated. It was of interest mainly due to the identity of the entity.

I had always liked the tall, sophisticated actor, George

Sanders, and I'd mentioned to my husband that some of his earlier pictures weren't worthy of his acting ability — referring to one just seen on television that Tuesday morning. Later, I read in the paper that he had committed suicide some time Monday evening. Tuesday night I was saying my prayers, which included beneficial words for earth-bound spirits, when there was a loud whack on the wall at the head of my bed. I jerked forward and turned around, but there was nothing I could see that would have caused such a sound. My intuition suggested it might be the movie actor, as he would be definitely still close to our world, if a suicide. But reasoning refused to accept that a famous star might want to contact an unknown, developing psychic.

By Wednesday morning, curiosity overcame me, and I sat to write before going to class. When I told my teacher about it, she seemed to think it was quite possible that it could have happened as I related it. This was the message from John:

"It was the spirit of earth-bound George Sanders trying to get your attention. No harm intended. It was because of your interest in him."

I never thought the day would come when I would refuse to acknowledge these spirit raps that so convinced me of our immortality. But a harrowing experience in another town resulted in my complete rejection of such physical evidence.

Possessed

*F*or three years we had been making long trips to our retirement center where we get our food and medical care. Since I don't like to drive very far, I thought it might be wise to settle nearer to everything we would need access to in our old age. We decided on another city — which shall be nameless. But those involved will recognize the events that were probably unknown outside our small group.

I was almost certain this would be my final move. But I stayed only three months, and then I was compelled to leave by a strange set of circumstances.

I had picked the place with great care. We had a nice apartment with a pool, and it was within five minutes of the center and the church. The latter had a good study course, guest speakers, and a discussion session that sounded ideal for furthering knowledge.

But I discovered that when I asked a question of the minister, she flung it back at me with another query, or else relegated it to a student or church official. This was disconcerting since I wasn't prepared to *give* answers — I *wanted* them. So I decided this was not sufficient for me, and I'd go home and get replies from my own writing.

Rose (my name for our minister), left for the summer during the next month, and a class was started so I could have something to attend while waiting for the fall courses to start.

I'll never forget Gary, the friendly man who set it up for me. We often talked about psychic matters after the meetings. In the middle of a conversation, he would come out with a sudden revelation of something he could see in my past or the present.

For the first few times a regular teacher was with us. But he left on account of illness in the family, and there was no one else to take over. It was like a curtain dropped in front of me, and I could no longer see as well clairvoyantly. I soon realized this was because Bea, one of the group, had abruptly developed the ability to do automatic writing. And then she announced that a guide had kept her awake all night talking to her.

I was fully aware that she might be in trouble. I hadn't read much about possession, because it was a frightening subject, but I did know the danger signals. Marie, an advanced student, said Bea was also giving wrong information. I'd acquired some words on the subject and wanted to read a few of the sentences to Bea. But she didn't appear to be listening to any of us — just hearing that commanding inner voice.

This was what was disclosed to me: "Clairaudience is less tiresome than the handwriting method of transmission, but it requires a more intense endeavor, because you must be able to rule out the unwanted entities who might try to speak to you. Unless the person is evolved enough to overcome this, it could be a problem. . . . Your means of communication is better protected by long use and your improved receptibility, besides our better control, due to more experience in dealing with you in this respect.

"Bea has indeed been unduly influenced by the entity claiming to be her guide. This is what we warn against as to psychic pursuits and their dangers. She has gone into it too fast. Your development has been slow but safe. She was not alert to the inherent possibilities of invasion. This can be relieved by the prayers of the group for her, and her insistence that the being leave at once."

Why was I exposed to this? To show me that I should not ask for specific psi activities until it was established that I was ready? Or to be able to tell others about the hazards from first-hand experience? I suspect it was a bit of both.

Here is a further account of what happened, as expressed by Marie in a letter to me after I had left the city: "Following the last class you went to, Bea threw herself back in the chair and, with hands out in front of her, appeared to go into a trance.

"She kept repeating, 'This is not Bea talking; it is someone else speaking for her. Don't touch me. I am the chosen one.' There were more odd things. We all put our hands on her, trying to calm her down. But by that time she'd scared the dickens out of us, and we went home worrying about her.

"Two or three days later, her friend Jan got a call from Bea at the hospital, telling her not to worry, that she didn't have a nervous breakdown, but had gone into a coma. She said her guide didn't want her to have any medicines or to sleep, and he kept waking her up.

"When she was released from the hospital, she went right back to class at the church. Now if that isn't unwise, I don't know what is! If I'd had that close a call, I would have stayed away — at least until my resistance and health were built up.

"Her husband finally heard about it all, as Bea showed him her writings and talked a lot about it. Well, the papers were torn up, and she is being sent to a psychiatrist. Her husband doesn't want anyone from the church in their home. Only Jan has any contact with her."

I found all these events were just the prelude to trouble for me. I had been pressured by Jay to go back to the Cape area, where he had worked before. He got a job over there and began to commute. The way things were going, I finally decided it would be best to move.

We bought a new mobile home, and I discovered it had numerous noises due to the contraction and expansion of the wood interior and metal exterior, especially when the weather was sunny or windy. But in the calm of the night, I began to hear sporadic raps on my sliding closet doors. A few times every night I woke up, and it took me about an hour to get back to sleep. I felt as if some of the bad effects of the town I'd just left had followed me. I knew that fear or thoughts of unwelcome spirits can attract them to you, and mine stayed with me for almost three months. I used all the affirmations in the books, and all I'd been told, but none worked. I sought advice from psi friends and ministers, but the sources they gave were ridiculous. Two said it was a relative. None of mine would do such an inconsiderate thing. Besides, they could have done it years ago when I started all this, so why wait till now? Then another gave a wild description of a man who had lost his thumb and was a writer. This just enhanced my fears, and I refused to do any writing from then on. The few times I had tried, I got the ensuing counsel:

"An unknown one has seen your light. As a psychic, you have acquired this by now, so he is trying to get through to you the easiest way known. Pray for all earth-bound souls to seek the God-Light that will lift them to higher levels in the astral world where they belong. By this effort you could gain stature, though we know it is hard on you to have sleep disturbed. If you cannot do this by yourself, we will assist you . . . . Do not indicate in any way that you are intimidated. It is not possession, just interference. You have tried your best. Be assured that this is endured effort that will be duly recorded."

Finally, someone must have impressed on my mind what to do, because it occurred to me to buy some earphones to put on when I slept. This worked fine, and though not too comfortable, I got used to it. Then I was inspired to a greater extent to take off the doors. They weren't needed, and I'd have more room to get at my clothes. Jay put them behind the sofa in the living room; but the taps continued there. This annoyed me, so we got permission to put them in a storage room at the mobile home park.

The last psychic I consulted said the spirit was a man who had worked on the doors. That made sense, and showed why he stayed with them and never awakened me after they were taken out of my room. Then my own communicant conveyed to me that the entity was electrocuted while cutting the doors with a defective power tool. He felt cheated of life, and so bothered those who lived on. It was added that he was obstinate about leaving. Well, I can certainly agree with that! But he met his match in me, because I was not about to leave my new home despite his vexing ways.

During the year, I received a note from Gary which mentioned that Bea's "evil entity was cast out," and that she appeared back to normal in every way and still attended classes.

Now that it is all over, I look back on it as a frightful way of learning that we can encounter such disturbing forces, and that we need to be made aware of how to cope with them.

A Return

J knew Gary was ill at times when I was at Rose's, but I had no idea it was cancer. Nor did he then, I'm sure. After I had moved, I wrote to thank him for all he had done. It was May of the next year before I got a long letter from him.

By then I was channeling past lives for those at the church, so I decided to ask about Gary's. I knew he did not believe in reincarnation, but I would not have related it to him if there was anything displeasing. What was disclosed was another of those strange pictures that seem to be put together like a jigsaw puzzle. The first part was only a small piece moved into place by Chou Wen Lee:

"The association with him, though brief, was meant to make you see the truth of dreams. You were married to him in a past life. Not to be in this one — though attraction felt. Both of you were psychic then in Babylon."

Months before I met Gary, I'd had a dream about a man who looked just like him. The substance of it was that I'd be very close to him, and that he had been married. A few days later, I found a picture in a paper of a minister who had a remarkable resemblance. Jokingly, I had disclosed all this to Gary, who surprised me by saying he'd been married before, and that he had wanted to be a preacher.

So now I thought this story would amuse my good friend. But I was unprepared for the manifestations that unrolled in the succeeding communications.

". . . A whole cloud of sadness came over me, and a great awareness within. My birthplace was Babylon, New York, September 18, 1914; and I was an orphan, vintage of World War I, at about three years of age. . . .

"The spiritual attraction cannot separate people, because of the one binding force of universal power. I love my God — the infinite wisdom which we share. Our psychic natures are God-given as channels of help for our fellow man. I approach each day with a deeper appreciation of the sacredness of His trust.

"My spiritual relationship with you must never wane, but wax to greater lives, though separate, for both of us. I feel your strength and prayers. The best to you and yours, and bless you always."

My first reaction to this lovely letter was that I had picked up Babylon by telepathy, because I didn't recall he had told me this. But a month later, another writing pinpointed it all too closely to accept it in this way. Also, I noted the further oddity that he was born in my birth year and on my husband's month and day.

In his next letter, the first week of June, he presented his attitude on previous lives, and brought up other things I felt I must reply to at once.

". . . I'm not completely against reincarnation. I just find more arguments against it. I'm open-minded, but am too foggy these days, with my weight at 119 pounds, to get into the intricacies just now. I was glad to get your message. Only take eighty percent of what your guides give you as true. None of the great mediums ever bank on more than that.

"Please explain what happens to your developed, material spirit body at transition, and what happens to the spirituality and individuality of the person. . . ."

I had supposed Gary was informed on this, but evidently he hadn't been able to read about it as I had. I considered the fact that I could answer the question with my own logical reasoning, but decided I should call on my Master Teacher. And most assuredly, the words chosen were better than any I could have consciously produced.

I did not include the first three paragraphs in my letter to him . . . for obvious reasons. Besides, he still had hope, as expressed when he wanted us to pray for him at church . . . "so I can live to do mankind some good."

The writing started in this way: "To help Gary is most urgent, since he needs to know the answers while there is still time. He has God in his life now, and he is to be taken soon.

"His mission here will be working with lost souls. He was one much of his life, due to being an orphan when so young, and to his many wanderings.

"Reincarnation disbelief will change when he arrives here. Then he will know it was not just a happenstance that you two were united in Babylonia, the country. That he was born in Babylon, the city in New York, was not only by chance, and should have made him recall the past. You were meant to cross his path again to bring this truth to him; and to aid him at the end, as he did for you in your last hours. This was caused by your not having faith in the after-life, which he knew to be a fact, since he had astrally projected into this other sphere of consciousness."

This last observation was unusual, as it seemed to me there were other ways I could have been convinced of what he had done for me. The main portion of the message continued:

"The astral part of the body at transition is more easily attuned if the person was prepared by teachings on earth. The entity has the ability to get a glimpse of the other dimension before passing. Its beauty is so great that many smile with joy at the sight. Those who are unconscious, due to drugs or coma, are left to sleep for a while in the haven of rest we have. It resembles a receiving ward, but not like the hustle and rush of your hospitals.

"There is love here, directed toward every soul, that he may awaken with a sense of security and awareness of the Divine Presence being manifested just for him.

"The individual realizes he still possesses his same mind and body, but it is the astral or spirit form that has left the old, physical shell behind. This new self is able to think and remember all that happened prior to his passing.

"Whether or not you acknowledge reincarnation does not matter. Know only that you live eternally in God's home, regardless if it be in heavenly continuance and progression, or in further lives on earth. You can select either as your way to evolve toward the Divine Light that leads to your reunion with God, your Maker."

I never did get a response to this, and I perceived that he must have become more seriously ill or passed on. I wrote Jill, the only one who could tell me, but had no answer from her.

On Sunday, August 5, I dreamed I saw Gary and remembered his blue eyes very clearly. Two weeks later, on August

19, also a Sunday, I sat down to write, but I felt such a restlessness that I just puttered around. It must have been a gradual realization, but I became intuitively aware of the possibility of Gary's presence there with me. The hair on my arms stood up (this means confirmation) but I couldn't see anything . . . as I never can. I began to pray for him, and after a while the sensation disappeared.

In October, I finally heard from Jill. She said she had mislaid my letter but found it when she cleaned out her desk. She wrote that Gary had died during the summer, but she didn't know when. It was after June, as she had seen him then. That was the month I had sent my last letter to him, so he must have gotten it. I asked her to please find out exactly what the date was, and told her why I wanted to know. A month later, her note gave the time as July 1.

The first of July was on a Sunday. On the first Sunday, a month later, he had reached me in the dream. (This would have been after his needed sleep "in the haven of rest.") On the third Sunday, I had the feeling that he was with me. Was this just chance? By choosing the holy day, wasn't he trying to show me that he now knew there were no coincidences in the realm of spirit? I believe so, and that he returned on days that would remind me of the "spiritual relationship" that we had.

What Became Of Donnie?

This is one time when I would like to use the real name. I haven't changed it much, but I must, because it is so personal. I wouldn't even print it, but I hope somehow if I do, and he sees it, I will hear from him again. Or maybe someone who recognizes the circumstances will realize that here is a soul crying out for understanding and try to help him.

He is a distant relative, and I am concerned as to what may have happened to him. I have written many times since his last letter of January, 1972, but no answer. I also asked the family to please tell me if anything is wrong, but I've been put off by vague replies. Was he really "cracking up," or have they been after him with a "straight jacket"?

I met him only once when we visited the relatives. He was a likeable, rather obese young man who also had an interest in the psychic. We talked all afternoon and had great rapport.

After that I received just two letters from him. They were so fascinating I've saved them all this time. I feel an urge to share them, as they show so well the heights and depths to which we can go in this study. The dream analysis is included here, because it all ties in with his experiences. The first letter was in November of 1971.

". . . I have been busy with a course in mind control. Part 1 teaches you to relax your body and still your mind, to get down to the alpha-theta regions of brainwave activity. Part 2 tells you what to do after you get there. For instance, to use visualization techniques to acquire anything you want, to go to sleep or stay awake without pills, to control pain and habits like over-eating, smoking, and other little things.

"In Part 3, things really start to get way out. You learn to project your consciousness into inanimate matter, such as plant or animal life. This is to help you to find lost articles, and to detect abnormalities in your car, plants, animals, or other things. The clincher is the last two exercises: the creation of a laboratory deep in your mind and the introduction into this lab of a male and a female counselor. They may be extensions of your own intelligence, and they are supposed to have access to all knowledge that is, was, or will be. When I saw mine, I was somewhat repulsed, because there was a huge brain in place of a head, no skin, and large yellow and black eyes. My instructor says if I don't like it, I can just say, 'Be gone,' and it will go. But I may not continue on to the last portion unless this gets straightened out. In Part 4, you find out how to project your consciousness into other humans, to discover any abnormality that may exist in their bodies, and hopefully, to help them. I've tried to do this, but had no success, probably because I haven't finished the course yet. You can take all or any part of it as many times as you like.

"For about four years I have been going through periods of depression that were becoming more frequent and longer lasting. Since I first started this study, I haven't had one bad day. I have lost thirty pounds, stopped biting my nails, and am a calmer, less anxious person.

"The method of relaxation begins by having you count

down from 10 to 1, and then picture pleasant, restful scenes. Then the count is shortened to 5 to 1, and 3 to 1. During the end of the course you get into and out of the proper area of the mind by the method best suited to your own needs.

"I have to go the full route: relax the body part by part from the scalp to the toes; then withdraw my consciousness upward from the toes. In one of the exercises, after you are relaxed and down to the alpha level, the instructor directs you to imagine your toes are not part of your body, and so on. But he never goes any higher than the knees.

"I decided to try it on my own and go all the way up to the top of my head. When I get all the way up, I say, 'I'm going to withdraw my consciousness from the top of my head,' and everything suddenly snaps into focus just behind and a bit above the bridge of my nose. I'm big and I'm little; I'm here and I'm there, all at the same time. It's a great but very strange feeling and just about impossible to describe.

"But this is not the ultimate; there is something else. If I continue to relax my mind after everything comes into focus (instead of meditating or working on some project related to the course), I soon get a feeling of trying to squeeze upward through a hole that's just a little too snug for me. I got through the hole one time, and I was aware of being on my bed and yet somewhere else also. When I came out of it, I was able to check on what I saw, and it was all just that way. I've never been able to get back, and it seems the harder I try, the less I succeed. Honest to goodness, you'll send someone after me with a net and a straight jacket . . . !'"

Donnie, did the head go away? Or did you get back up into that hole again . . . maybe once too often? I wish I knew, or could get in touch with you, but I can't. So let me go on to the dream, which had unusual imagery, was fairly well interpreted, and may have triggered precognition on my part.

"Several weeks ago I had a marvelous, but frightening, dream. I wish you were closer so I could talk to you sometimes . . . . I dreamed that my cousins, Janie and Joe, and I were on an island. They are very close to me, so I was not surprised to know that we were there together. We were walking along a beach where the sand was in mounds, something like graves. We came to the last mound where we buried a box in the sand. I can't remember what was in the box, but we all agreed it was supposed to be improved when the three of us came back to get it.

"Then I left them there and boarded a sailboat. I climbed up into the rigging so I could feel the wind blowing in my hair and on my face. I knew when I left the shore that the boat was just going to sail around in a circle, and that I would never even lose sight of the island.

"The ocean was full of boats; most of them were hazy and indistinct in the distance, but I came very close to one other boat which carried a woman. I didn't recognize her, and when I woke up, I couldn't recall her face. I noticed that the water was not clear, it was a little choppy, and there were a few pieces of debris floating around.

"Just a little less than half way around the circuit the boat was taking, I looked down into it and saw a young man smiling up at me. I knew who he was instantly because, up until his death in Vietnam last year, he was an old friend of my brother's. I asked him why he was there, to which he replied, 'I'm here to help you steer this boat.' I lazily hung there in the rigging, wondering what this was all about. Then I realized I was not in a boat but lying in my bed.

"I was aware that I had been having a dream, but I was not yet fully awake. This happens frequently to me, and in this semi-awake state I 'dream' an interpretation of the previous dream, or at least get some guidance in this direction. But this time I woke up sooner and had to interpret some of it myself. I think these sleep images come to us in terms we accept and understand.

"The box and mounds I'm not sure of, though I feel the latter refer to my life in the past or now. I set sail on the ocean of life, knowing that I would come back to the island and my cousins. I started before they did, since they are younger than I. The murky water may indicate that my life or thinking is not as clear as it could be, and the choppiness shows that my journey will not be a smooth one; though I saw no big waves. The debris must be bad habits that need cleaning up. The woman who sailed so close to me is evidently important, but since I can't recall who she was, I don't know what role she will play in my life.

"The part about my brother's departed friend, Tom, waiting to help guide my life, really raised my hackles. I don't know just how he is going to do this, or what I'm supposed to do about it. I haven't had any more dreams about him. But while I am writing this, I get the distinct sensation of something standing at my back. Perhaps it's just that I'm recalling the dream; maybe I'm imagining things, or maybe I'm cracking up! It's strange and a little frightening. . ."

I have tried to analyze Donnie's dream, and this is the way I see it: By taking mind control studies, he had enlarged his view of the voyage of his life, symbolized by his going up into the rigging of the sailboat. Going to sea was a sign of his desire to break with his family, which he had already done by refusing to live with his father. Obviously, this contributed to a great deal of emotional repression for Donnie — as seen by the mounds of sand which he said resembled graves. Also, he did not realize that the box he buried was a covered-up wish (to be fulfilled) concerning the death of his father. Then conditions would "be improved," and he could go back home. A box is known to refer to a coffin or death wish; and besides, he was boxed in by inner and outer forces.

He was sure he would just sail around the island, because he had a subconsious knowledge that it was but a cycle of his life that he would be able to complete and then return to his close relatives. The muddy water represented unseen, limiting constraints. He did not recall the woman in the boat since he wanted to shut out the idea that she could be the only woman he had cared about in four years: "I had become very fond of her. Just a few weeks before Christmas, she told me she was engaged to a man she'd met only three weeks before. I was shocked, hurt, and grieved, and I'm sure this will alter my whole outlook on everything. . ." In November, he had tuned in to the fact that he would come very close to the woman; but only symbolically saw that the choppy water (another man) would push her away from him.

The brother's dead friend may have been trying to help Donnie steer through that phase of his existence, by way of the dream or mental guidance.

I had sent a writing about the meaning of it all, and this was part of the answer in his last letter: "You said that the box was to warn me of a death in the family that would change my life. I certainly hope it's for the better. . ."

We heard that his father died in the summer of the next year. But there is still no word of what became of Donnie.

*T*he next pages are counselings for me and others. They also include observations about God as Spirit, prayer, the soul, meditation methods, and color meanings.

When I first heard that the defects we dislike in others are the ones we have ourselves, I thought it was too illogical that we would allow our actions to resemble those we judged so harshly. But I found it was like the time I went to the dentist with an apparent toothache. He informed me that I had been gritting my teeth, which I flatly denied. Then I went home and caught myself doing it.

I didn't realize I'd been abhoring pettiness in others until it seemed to loom up in so many of the people I wanted as friends. With my new insight, I looked within and wondered if this trait was one I had harbored. I asked about this in a writing and got the following helpful advice:

"Do not become involved with those who seek to belittle you, as you will not only be upset, but may take on karma from them, which means, your not being able to tolerate the weaknesses of the persons could result in your having to return to work it out again. Your destiny this time was to be subjected to the trivialities of some, since you were once that way. The need is not that you must stay around them (if it can be avoided), but to show you how small and warped they are.

"Be always alert to these pitfalls: The people who like to drag you down to their level; the ones who are envious of your achievements; and those who have no interest in what you are trying to do that would help them. How do you counteract this negativity? Visualize them surrounded by the White Light of Truth. This will aid you also to rise above their injurious ways."

Dissatisfaction is the best stimulation for new growth in wisdom. If you are bored, it could be because you are not content with what little knowledge you have absorbed. Reach out and try to learn more about yourself and the whole, big universe in which you live. Accept only what you feel you can assimilate. Put aside the rest as being beyond your powers to digest, but feel no inferiority. We all learn at different levels.

To worry about things working out is a waste of energy that is essential for the betterment of true insight. Rationalizing as to what should be done is not the way to approach problems. It is easier to be impressed with the truth by relaxing and turning it over to the Indwelling Mind. Don't weaken your hard-won battle with depression and lack of faith. There has to be more to life than misery, because it plagues everyone.

I sought more enlightenment about God, as I was confused, because of the many beliefs to which I'd been subjected.

"God is Spirit and dwells within you, as He does in everyone and everything. He is the Creator of all life, intelligence, and power. He does not exist in a visible body and rule the heavens as a strict overseer waiting to punish you. His role is that of a loving Father who wishes you to draw on the goodness which He can supply.

"You were created with this in mind — that you would come back to the One, perfect as He is perfect; like unto Him in all respects. This is why you must achieve that ideal by many of life's evolutions, so that progress is swifter. Even though the learning is arduous, it is most fulfilling. The purifying processes are accomplished in the return to the higher spheres.

"Without Spirit, you are unguided, unloved and uninspired, in the purest sense of the words. God as Spirit is the Source of all that is true and right with the world. So chart your course in His direction."

I was given a summary of some basic principles by my Master Teacher: "Being in harmony with your fellow man is a first precept. Then determine if you have forgiven those who have abused you. The importance of this is noted in the Christ's words when he was crucified: 'Father, forgive them, for they know not what they do.' The third thing to learn is to conquer impatience with others. Their viewpoints may not coincide with yours, but they have the right to their beliefs also.

"These are only three . . . more will be given. But work on them, as they need to be rectified for your further progress."

I think about them often, and realize they are indeed my weaknesses. Sometimes, instead of counting to ten, I say, "Patience, harmony, forgiveness."

On the subject of prayer, I would like to give first this channeled comment, which contains many of the main concepts we should grasp:

"*Thy will be done* is the most holy pronouncement you can declare in your prayers to the Supreme Being. You must learn to trust His decisions as to what is right for you.

"Make your wishes for fulfillment constructive ones that can help you to develop your resourcefulness. These are not selfish beseechings, because you earnestly desire to improve yourself. Entreaties to enlarge your possessions, or your egoistic status are not acceptable to Him, however. So aim to keep the channels open for only the highest, finest and best to be considered for His approval.

"Do not misunderstand — this does not mean God ignores prayers that are from the heart, or that constitute a real necessity of any sincere soul. But one must learn to distinguish between the self-seeking and the self-uplifting. The difference is as night is to day, but only those steeped in the Goodness of God can be sure of the distinction between the two.

"To begin with, examine your motives: Are they aimed to produce the best that is in you? Are they also proposed to help others? Within and without, there is thus equalizing of the forces necessary to encourage you to progress toward the Holy Light and receive His benedictions."

The placement of the spiritual consciousness is at the top of the head. For that reason, we feel lifted up when we pray — if we are cognizant that this is the origin of all that is inspirational.

Prayers will be answered if you believe; unless you have somehow used the wrong approach. For instance, if you have any ill feelings toward another, ask first for self-help to eliminate these, before expecting self-good. It isn't that you have requested anything unessential, just keep trying to improve your awareness. Then all will be solved at the right time and under the best circumstances.

Always give thanks when there is a solution. This will make it easier for more benevolence to take place. You can also show satisfaction over a worthwhile project you have accomplished, and know it will further enlighten your mind's capacities; but do it with humility, not bragging.

Say your prayers in the last few minutes before going to sleep and your rest will be more peaceful. . . . Merely repeating words written by others, without concentrating on the meaning, does not result in much motivation. . . . Let go and let God take over to work it out for you. Be convinced the problems will be overcome.

Prayer is talking to God. Meditation is trying to contact Him by listening. Either way, we need to calm the outer mind and go to the inner stillness. Segregate the words of the psalmist: "Be still and know that I am God." Be still and know that I am. Be still and know. Be still. Each is a powerful thought.

"The wisdom of man is achieved by the activity of the soul, which was implanted in us because God thought we needed a superior guidance center to bring us closer to His image. The ability of the soul to influence us is dependent on our willingness to release it by the removal of our thoughts from the mundane and material. When this is done, we become renewed; with a more intense conviction of the value of self and others. Then much is accomplished, as ideals are extended and faith is stronger.

"Trust in other persons is an important part of soul expansion, for if you really believe in the sincerity of another, he will return the same to you. Faith breeds faith; doubt creates a doubter. The soul, or your more noble sense, tries to persuade you to liberate your mind to accept this better way of life. You are obviously benefitted if you do.

"The soul's endless journey takes it over hills and valleys of the human existence. Without the guiding power of the intuitional level of consciousness, the way is fraught with hazards to both the mental and physical body.

"Lift up your eyes and hearts and discover your higher self by prayer and meditation. Remember that the Eternal Spirit is trying to speak to you. After you have stilled the intellect, take a pencil and write what you feel He is attempting to tell you. The words of wisdom should amaze you, if you have pursued the proper approach.

"The soul is the more exalted part of your mentality — that elusive, non-measurable element that so baffles the investigators who want proof of all that is unknown or untouchable to them. It is an infinite, yet definite, portion of your self that abides with you from here to eternity. Treat it with care, nourish and let it grow. Don't stifle it with materialistic attitudes. It must have the Divine Light in order to flourish. Open the door of your mind and let the light come in. Knock, and ye shall enter. Seek, and ye shall find. Ask, and knowledge shall be given unto you."

Before entering into meditation, consider that learning to relax is really controlling your mind to surmount outer disturbances. It releases you from the confines of the physical, and propels you toward the acquisition of more elevated expressions.

This discipline is achieved by focusing attention on spiritual words. Making the mind a blank is not the answer, as some advocate. To fulfill, you must be filled with truthful affirmations that lead to the expansion necessary to reach the wisdom of the Spirit. However, too much concentration can cause the very tension you are attempting to relieve. So do it only for a short time at first. And also realize that what you have accomplished by the soul-searching needs to be applied to everyday activities.

There will be periods when you feel you are making no headway. But this may mean a new step is to be taken, so try to see only the light ahead — the understanding that will come.

When you are in possession of an illuminating idea, you can be assured that it has come from the Universal Mind, and you were attuned to it. Don't be afraid to seek the highest, for you will discover a new vitality of your whole being. You may become a channel and will be approached in whatever way is best, due to your stage of development. Answers to your queries are within you, just as God is. As you progress, these will be manifested through you, whether in visions, dreams, writing, drawing, or other inspired means.

These are procedures I have worked out from experience, and are a composite of many teachings. Use it as a guide until you find your own way of doing it. To choose a method that appeals to you personally is important, because if you are not comfortable in any phase of it, you will not gain the power necessary to propel yourself toward the summit of heightened awareness.

Meditation Methods

1. Sit in a straight chair with feet flat on the floor and hands in lap, palms up usually.

2. Say affirmations or a prayer. I like the one attributed to St. Francis of Assisi. Among the affirmations I use are the sentence from the 46th Psalm, already mentioned, and "The White Light of Truth surrounds me, protecting me from all negative thoughts or conditions."

3. Breathe rhythmically, pushing out stomach muscles when you inhale, and in when you exhale. Do this at least three times.

4. Visualize each part of you as relaxed, starting with the feet

and on up to the head. In time, just the thought can cause you to relax all over.

If you have a picture of the Master, gaze at the face, especially the space between the eyes. Then close your eyes and direct them to the center of your forehead.

Mentally project the universal word Om, which will focus attention and eliminate the intrusion of unwanted thoughts. Repeat it when necessary during psi activity. It is pronounced like A-um. The first letter is given out as you inhale, and the um as you exhale. Breathe slowly and in rhythm, until you feel ready for step seven. (In some classes the Om is spoken aloud. If you need this extra power, open the mouth for the Ah sound, and close it to get the hum of the last syllable. This way, it is all said as you exhale. Do it about seven times.)

At this point you can send out healing thoughts and prayers, begin to see images, or take up the pencil to write, draw, or compose music.

Close with a protective affirmation, such as the one given in step two.

The Light Method

Place a lighted candle on the table near your face.

Stare at the flame for about a minute.

Close your eyes and concentrate them on the center of the forehead. The flame should appear in your mind's eye.

Relax and see what begins to form.

You may observe several things, so be prepared to write them on paper in case you are forgetful. Since the eyes need to be kept closed, place the finger of the left hand over each line as it is recorded, so the writing won't run together.

The Meanings of Colors

All colors manifest physical, mental, or spiritual characteristics, whether seen clairvoyantly, used in healing, decorating, or worn as clothes. Colors are vibrations, so if some irritate you, it is no doubt because they don't suit you and will cause disharmony. To make it more generally interesting, I've used words to depict personality traits. The purest, strongest form of the color is given first. Duller ones indicate less desirable qualities. All descriptions have been analyzed as the most logical from various sources.

Red — energetic, optimistic, impulsive
    rose — loving, helpful
    dark — moody, restrained

Orange — ambitious, confident, contented

Yellow — intellectual, idealistic, artistic
    light — cautious, retiring
    dull — introspective, indecisive
    gold — spiritual, intuitional

Green — adaptable, sincere, determined
    light — sentimental, sympathetic
    dark — evasive, envious

Blue — loyal, calm, conscientious
    turquoise — impetuous, clever
    dark — self-sufficient, conservative

Violet — harmonious, meditative, creative
    lavendar — pleasant, but precise
    purple — proud, successful

Brown — practical, responsible
    dark — critical, shrewd

Gray — reserved, apathetic
    light — changeable, insecure
    dark — selfish, depressed
    silver — more refined and constant

Black — dignified, conventional, emphatic

White — high spirituality, perfection, peacefulness

I couldn't understand why so much importance was put on the word Truth in metaphysics, and why it was so often capitalized. Then I read the definition of it and found that: Truth is all that is in everything — the source, power, reality, mind, the infinite, the whole, goodness, spirit, ideals — all words used to describe God's attributes.

I feel as if I am overdoing it if I capitalize where it is not conventionally done that way. I know that metaphysicians accentuate many words by this means. But my newness to the study has me confused as to exactly which ones to stress, so I will try to limit this practice to those which allude directly to God or Christ. Sometimes in my writing, capitals were used for emphasis, and I have copied these as given, even though they may not be correct usage or consistent.

I believe the real meaning of the Truth came to me one Sunday when I went to a new church. It was strange the way the words on the program suddenly seemed to fluctuate. The names and quotations appeared to be different than when I had first glanced at them. I even compared my printed sheet with my husband's, as I thought maybe his was dissimilar. But both were alike. Then why did I feel that the words before me had varied from the way they were originally?

I think it all began when we sang "In the Garden." It was my favorite hymn. During the first verse I was suddenly overwhelmed with deep emotion, and my voice choked up so much that I had to shift to the lower range of notes. My eyes closed, because I knew it so well I didn't need to look at the words.

Even at the healing service, my eyes were still shut. I was vaguely conscious of voices and the organ playing, and I could see blue lights. When it was time for prophesies, I was the only one asked to stand up. I thought I was listening to what was said, but I didn't remember a word of it. Jay told me later what it was: "You are blessed; and you could be at the pulpit giving messages. You have a lot to contribute to the group. . . ."

I spoke to the minister after church, and I couldn't recall names of people we both knew. Nor could I tell where we were moving, which was nearby. I am forgetful at times, but this was too much.

After we returned home, I had difficulty thinking of what to do next. As we ate, Jay mentioned things that were said outside the building, but it was all hazy to me. It was very unsettling to be so out of focus.

Then it occurred to me — was it a touch of Cosmic Consciousness — an experience such as Bucke had described? I knew it could not be that great elevation noted in the lives of such men as Buddha, Moses, Jesus, Whitman, Emerson and others; but I did recognize the conditions as being some changed state of consciousness. I knew I'd had an uplifting to heights above ordinary realization . . . beyond the limits of the physical into the farther reaches of awareness.

I had prayed for a sign of where to go to further my development in this area. This must have been the way it was to be revealed to me.

I called on my Teacher for his insight: "It was an altered state, as you thought, but not Cosmic Consciousness. That occurs only for those who have acquired it through much meditation on the Lord's ideals. Also, service to others is necessary before true illumination of the Spirit can be forthcoming. This will be within your grasp if you dedicate yourself to God's Truth and Light."

The next unusual event that manifested itself was soon after a singularly psychic woman began to attend our church. Celia explained many novel ideas to me. Among these was a method of using water to replenish the energy that is drained after channeling is done. These were the words that led to the start of a whole new aspect of my evolvement:

"Praise the Lord that Celia has been brought to you to teach you things you needed to know through an earth soul. You can in turn help her, through your sensitivity to the records we keep here."

There followed revelations about two of her close relatives, and then one about my Grandmother Alice. I'd been told that she was psychic but had never mentioned it to the family. She was very spiritual, too, and I had felt especially drawn to her.

"Alice awaits you here. Be consoled that she wanted to speak to you of rewards of service to God, but she knew your karmic pattern and could not interfere. How her tears flowed for you, as yours do now, on viewing the anguish that was to be yours, from which she could not spare you. But now you can indeed join her on a higher plane, as we tried to tell you once before. Water . . ."

By this time, I was crying so much I needed to stop and get calmed down in some way, so I tried pouring tap water back and forth between two glasses ten times. I held the water in my mouth and gradually, from under my tongue, I began to detect a sweet taste. This was amazing to me that it worked, because I really hadn't expected it. (Oh, ye of little faith!) Anyway, I returned to my tablet of paper, and the ensuing sentences were recorded so swiftly that I had no time to comprehend their contents:

"The Father, Son, and Holy Spirit were visited upon you this day to lead you to the Christ. . . . (I suddenly felt faint and sick for a brief second.) Illness passes — a sign you've been touched by Christ. He will be with you now forevermore.

"The different taste of water was due to His blessing. Your words will come too fast to record. This is new faith given to you. God be with you." (All this was hastily scribbled in narrow, pointed letters, unlike the others. Then a star was drawn.)

"The Star of David will be with you now. The Guardian Angel, reincarnation of Biblical Moses, is to be your Teacher. He was known as The. . .ocrites — Theocrites, a wise philosopher of the Middle Ages."

When I had recovered from all this, I did some research and found the Star of David, formed by two interlaced triangles, was the emblem of Judaism, and a mystic symbol in the Middle Ages. It is also used to depict the soul and Oversoul (the Eternal Spirit).

Now for the odd coincidences — if you wish to call them that. But coincidence is really only strange because of the odds against its happening so often. I see it all as part of God's plan.

I was to give a talk at church one Sunday. (This was previous to the manifestation I've just described.) Since we were to use a Bible quotation, I decided to let the book open wherever it would. This happened to be at the Ten Commandments. I wondered why, as it did not pertain to my subject matter at all. Then I recalled how moved I had been by the recently reviewed film of *The Ten Commandments*. This led me to want to know more about Moses. When I reached the passage in Exodus 4:10, my eyes were unusually arrested by these paragraphs, which so graphically described my feelings about having to speak:

"And Moses said unto the Lord, O my Lord, I am not eloquent . . . but I am slow of speech, and of a slow tongue.

"And the Lord said unto him, who hath made man's mouth . . . have not I. . . .?

"Now therefore go, and I will be with thy mouth and teach thee what thou shalt say."

I put this in the preface to my speech, and I was at ease and untroubled by any difficulties of expression.

Besides the "chance" of my turning to this beneficial Scripture about Moses, weeks before I was told of his becoming my Teacher, it was unknown to me that the six-pointed star was connected with the Middle Ages. Theocrites says I cannot prove who he was because: "I . . . once Moses . . . came back as an obscure philosopher in that period between ancient and modern times. The date is not important, and it would be hard to find information on the name in any indexed reference. I was supposed to be an unrenowned entity in that life, to learn the humility of not being a well-known person. After that, I decided to try to assist others who were undistinguished to become recognized for their good works."

I hoped this was meant as encouragement for me, but I didn't feel it then, because that paragraph was produced very laboriously. The next day Chou Wen Lee was my transmitter.

"I come today, since new one has had trouble with adjustment to your mental tuning. As we write, he will pick up our method so he can have more success in the future. We will know when he is ready, so no more time will be wasted.

"All your Masters are still with you. Though we may seem to withdraw, yet we help at times, as I reappear now to speed up your phrases. Thus shall it be always for you. We step aside if one with more impetus can contact you. None of us wish to slow you down, since we have at last built up your confidence in us."

A week later, Theocrites spelled out his name and laconically stated: "I think we are ready to communicate now." It all flowed easily from the pencil, and some parts were more speedily written. He drew the Star of David at the end . . . and from that time on.

This account, and a few that follow, show cause for my self-improvement, but contain food for thought for anyone. It may seem to belong under guidance, but all of Theocrites' statements are so full of absolute truth that I prefer to put them together in this one chapter. In addition, I will separate each one by extra space, so they will be more distinguishable.

"Christ came to prepare the way for you to enter the kingdom of Heaven. Therefore be not blind to His teachings. 'Be ye also perfect as your Father in heaven is perfect.'

"These words were impressed on your consciousness when you were about to criticize someone. Since you can't claim perfection, there should be no notice taken of the lack in others. This abstaining will insure that words of understanding and goodwill shall be the only ones to leave your lips. Can you picture perfection in this way?

"You who want the earthly treasures in absolute alignment, should be able to manipulate your thoughts into the correct channels. This is a gentle chiding, a hope that it will aid you to curb any future indulgence in just tolerating rather than loving.

"If you truly love, as the Lord commands, you respond favorably to all conditions. No negative thinking, or outpouring of same, shall be possible. Follow then in His footsteps and live always in the Light of the Lord."

"Having an open mind produces more rapport with people who may appear to be difficult to deal with. Like so many things in the human element, harmony is something that is hard to achieve, because every personality has its own needs, desires, likes and dislikes. So there is naturally friction caused by the clash of ideas. When this occurs, then how you react is what is important.

"Do not return the same viciousness to the sender. This lowers you to his level, and makes you liable to his limitations, which could minimize your efforts to overturn the negativity and improve the effect by offering a more wholesome outlook. By replying in a light, constructive vein, you fend off the harassment and substitute the mildness and benevolence necessary to establish calmness and peace.

"In theory, this sounds fine, but in practice, it is less easy to do? True; but practice does make perfect, and if you can succeed once, the next time it will be smoother and there will be more accord between you."

"Let us present more on the truths of Spirit unfolding within you, in the form of enobling your nature to the point where personal problems will no longer exist. True erudition is knowing when to listen and when to speak. Having a curiosity about all things is a way to learn, but keep the mind receptive to the intake of the emotional expressions as well. The ways and means are not as valuable as the concern over whether you are feeling His Presence with you.

"Real truth perceives the difference between the practical and the ideological. Without aspirations we would be like a boat without a rudder. And the love of our fellow man exceeds the casual approach we give to fundamental reasons for being and doing.

"Thus, the purpose of living is seen to be trying to attach ourselves to the changeless realities of God's principles; not just the furtherance of general knowledge of the intellect. However, an equalization of both can create an enriching attunement."

Someone was acclaiming the idea of self-expression through analyzing ourselves and our experiences. While this may help in therapy cases, it did not appeal to me as a method of acquiring spirituality. I directed this to Theocrites in order to get his version, which was brief, but to the point.

"This is like raking over the coals of the past. While we learn from our mistakes, to dwell on them by repetition is to affirm rather than deny. And we must deny error, because there is only one Power — the Goodness of God. God is All, so anything else is the absence of good; as darkness is lack of light. By affirming this truth we can erase any appearance of error, which is really incorrect thinking."

"This is uppermost today: the will to accomplish is a worthy endeavor, but allow time to absorb what you have learned through study, work and experience. By this means only can unity of purpose be fulfilled. Having concepts without deeds is like producing flowers with no leaves; and nature does not evolve in that manner.

"It is true that ideas must come before actions can take place. But they must grow from the ground up. The basic elements, the roots, stems, and leaves, contain the properties that will enable the resulting flower of truth to give forth the pollens that will generate future good works.

"The power of a thought is the result of the gradual process of its growth into the higher consciousness — the flowering segment of the mind."

"Measure all things according to what the Bible says about interest in the spiritual gifts. They are declared to be of God if the acquisition is within the limits of His perfection. Be therefore cognizant of what is transmitted to you. Is it worthy of His name, conforming to natural laws and His spiritual laws?

"Only you, in your intuitional state of consciousness, can determine this. Teachers can judge by their standards, but all are progressing at various levels, so what seems right to one is wrong to another. Thus, do not be disturbed about how you get the Word, because it is the content that matters.

"If there are mistakes, the discernment you have attained could detect them. This is where the conscious mind helps also, by logically checking the authenticity of your statements. Though it needs to be sidetracked during reception, it should be put back on the mainline when the material is read over afterwards.

"We confirm the value of your work, but then we are only Teachers too. Do you believe in your abilities as rewarding? The ego is put aside in this self-evaluation. Make your decisions on all things based on His Will for you and everyone concerned."

This had a most unusual ending: "Telling all you know about the Lord — His revelations, His rules, and His reasons for man's behavior — is your mission on earth in this lifetime. Yours is not to prophesy, but to tell the truth and banish the lie. (Poetic ... but it doesn't allow for the predictions I was given that came true!) So many know not what to believe. We must teach them the realistic meanings of the Word of God as we understand it.

"The truth you shall always seek and share. Your soul has longed for that all your years of living, now and in the past. And at last it can be told, because we have been able to upraise your mind to be receptive to this. Determined acceptance on your part to give us the time is all that is needed. Rewards will be great, on earth and in heaven ... the eternal reality. Impressive, intuitional guidance in all your affairs shall be forthcoming. So be wise, as we know you are, and admit the words of God into your consciousness.

"With these welcoming thoughts, you have been invited to

join the flock of the Holy Shepherd, the Christ Jesus. Thy holy servant and Master Teacher, Theocrites."

This great one was alluding to himself as a servant to me? This was surely an unexpected declaration of humility, and one from which I could learn. It was evident he had gained it when he became that little-known philosopher in the Middle Ages.

These were his words on spiritual understanding: "Resolute compliance with the Lord's hope for all mankind — learning to love, forgive, have patience, tolerance, and zeal for His undertakings — is the lesson you must ascertain. Being wholly immersed in His spirituality is achieved through the injection of His wisdom into your intellectual brain. This then has to be transferred to the more elevated self by meditation and prayer.

"The path to true upliftment is not just easy steps up a ladder. The heavy, material feet cannot be raised to the next level until so moved by the higher consciousness, which knows whether you have assimilated enough of the truth to be able to fully commit yourself to the Infinite Intelligence.

"Only by loving your fellow man can you enjoy the real fruits of Divine Wisdom. Have compassion for those who cannot rise above their physical infirmities. Listen to them; yet try to go beyond sympathy to affirmation that nothing except goodness and wholeness can enter the bodies of those who entrust their souls and minds to His keeping.

"How is this done? Simply by opening your heart to draw in His blessing — much as you gave your love to your earthly mate. This was not difficult to do, so why should it appear such an insurmountable step to accept God's Love? Just because He can't be seen doesn't mean He isn't there beside you, eternally with and within you. Even when your loved ones are far from you, their loving presence is felt by you, is it not?

"Then absorb into your being the All-Goodness — the Power that can lift the illness, the despair, the heartache from your shoulders and onto His. He will not feel the burden. Christ stumbled under the weight of the Cross He carried, but God lifted Him."

The next was a rather profound dissertation dealing with our subject: "The reception of truth into your consciousness is the way to open the door to the many mansions promised by the

Son. The Father has room for all of you in His house and heart. But you must earn the privilege to enter therein.

"Have all the students of a college keys to their classrooms? Only the teachers, who have studied long and arduously, are given this exclusive access to the inner halls of learning. And this is rightfully so, because whosoever accepts the Word of God must also be able to live it to the fullest. It is not enough to say 'I know'; you must say, 'I do.' The letters of the laws are perfect, but are you who try to follow them perfect?

"The intellectual gain, pursued parallel with the spiritual, is the best way of high attainment. Balance in all areas of expression is necessary. Truth is not easily found — the Ultimate Reality, that is. There are many half-truths within easy reach of the indolent student.

"To recognize the real truth takes years of deep penetration into the intuitional recesses of the mind. Then you begin to see the light at the end of the dark tunnel of progress. And you come out into the glorious sunlight of God's Universe and behold the shining alabaster of His Mansions, which are to be the dwellings of all seekers and followers of His Truth."

Here was a combination of hope, faith, and love interwoven with a skill my brain alone could not have produced: "Hope for a brighter future has been our desire since man's beginning on earth. This hope, that continually bolsters our faith, is the haven of true inspiration, because, without hope, we would be deprived of incentive and the will to know how to work God's principles into our everyday lives.

"Have faith that He will guide you in all you do. When all else fails, His wishes for your welfare are ever-present and sustaining. The part you play is cancelling all doubts you may have as to His Power to bring out the best in you. When confidence is infused, the All-Good can express itself, and accord between the inner and outer selves is attained. Faith requires an intense allegiance to the highest, finest and best in life, which is God's inspiration eternally burning its luminous flame to show you the way.

"The manifestations of gifts of the Spirit are a form of proof of the Lord's Power. But real faith is belief without evidence. We do not minimize the value of such outward expressions of His omnipotence, but wish it to be understood that the utmost satisfaction is reliance on His Love — the greatest offering of all.

"Learn to give and receive this goodness, and more will be added. Faith can move mountains, but love is the force behind it which lifts the first rock. Conscientiously storing up devotion gives a surplus to draw upon when the supply of faith runs low. It is not the easiest thing to do — to adopt truths without clearly defined facts of their existence. That is why we say love should go along with faith; for, without it, faith is more difficult to retain."

I had to look up two things after this reception, as I did not consciously recall the knowledge. I thought Euripides was a writer, but found him to be also classed as a philosopher. Other facts, besides the Dead Sea Scrolls, show the teachings of the Essenes were the same as Jesus used in His preaching.

"The wisdom of the ages was promulgated by the instructions of the philosophers who were the truly enlightened ones — Plato, Pythagoras, Euripides, Socrates, Aristotle, Origen, and others. Their concepts are being re-examined now at a time when they are much needed. The logic, aligned with the consciousness of One Creator, and the pursuit of awareness of the problems and solutions needed for man's soul growth — all this was given consideration in the presentation of their theories.

"Just so were modern-day men inspired to manifest their beliefs and to interpret the Bible in words more understandable to the people. These changes are no more radical than those made by the early Christian Church, which ruled out much that was taught by Jesus and the Essenes. Being critical of the meanings given by scholars of any age is therefore a maligning pactice that should cease.

"Unity of thought is necessary — not more divergent viewpoints — there are so many which are perplexing man today, besetting him with doubts and uncertainties as to what is really true. Metaphysicians are on the right path. They have gained the answers through contemplation and seeking from the Ultimate Source."

In a psychic's message for me, it was stated that I was a mother many times in the past. Then came this cryptic phrase: "Motherhood is symbolic." I sought the interpretation from Theocrites, and he said it referred to the compassion I have for others. He continued: "Do not feel you failed in this lifetime because of harsh treatment of sons. That was for their own good — that they might meet the world's ways with fortitude.

"The weak mothers are those who accede to the child's every whim in order to be well-liked. But the wise child knows he is loved, even though punished, because the truly loving parent disciplines the young one, that he may grow up to follow the straight and narrow path that leads to the eternal light that is God's guidance."

Because it is so beautifully expressed, I'd like to include a copy of a letter I got from my older son, when he had incurred the rigors of service life after being drafted.

"Dear Mom, I did remember that today was Mother's Day. Through the week I considered how I should acknowledge the occasion. Greeting cards were readily available, but that was too easy. I looked through a book of quotations to find one, but none were appropriate to my thoughts.

"The time of attachment has since passed. I'm out to cut my own path through the jungle and establish my own settlement with the machette that was partially tempered at home. I am most grateful for the training and inspiration which I was given, and which I received consciously and even unconsciously at the time.

"I am hoping that the future finds me doing works and deeds that I can be proud of — perhaps you will be too — it is your consolation if so."

There was a transcription that was short but forceful. Most of the words came to me before they were written down, and much faster than I could possibly realize their meaning.

"We have a more alert, more intellectual matrix of young idealists today. They are breaking away from the conformity of their elders and molding their own concepts of life. This is being done by intuitional introspection of theories once heralded by the ancient philosophers, and also by examining the truths of the Biblical leaders.

"These young people are the forerunners of the New Aquarian Age, and will precede and peacefully prepare the way for the return of the Christ. With this armor protecting them, they will be among the ones saved in the purification that will be prior to this greatest of all events since the ascension of the

Master.

"Be prepared, all those who disbelieve, for this too shall come to pass, and the time is nearer than many comprehend. So decide now to lift up your eyes and see the glory that is His. You who know and study His Truth are favored in the sight of the Lord and do show forth His handiwork, until the day when He shall come again to encompass about Him the faithful who shall rise up with Him to the kingdom of heaven. Oh come all ye faithful, sing in exaltation, for ye shall see His face before you and feel the nearness of His Presence."

"The mental accomplishment we achieve determines our place in the plan of the Universal Mind. Each of us is part of the overall manifestation of the world as it will be, so we should be inspired to do our best in contributing to the welfare of the place we inhabit. It is our only home in the here and now, and we must guard it against any negative conditions. Our unity of purpose is of great importance, and every one of us should see ourselves as a vital component of the Divine Ideal.

"Time for us can run out only in the sense that we allow it to, in respect to our efforts on the earth plane. There is no time, per se, in the eternal spheres, so why should we be tied to it here? Do as much as you can each day, then release the unfinished business to the next period of endeavor. This unloads frustrations of the spirit, which can upset the equilibrium required for your wholeness of being. Do not hinder fulfillment of the Lord's design for you who are an integral part of all that is and shall be."

"The day will come when the trials and testings are over. Then the picture will clear, and no longer will you be looking through the glass darkly. The decisions, meanwhile, must be yours. Only you can make the moves that will bring you the most happiness. Others can advise, but your soul knows what is best, and this is the voice to heed. The Spirit within wants what you do to be the right thing, but it will not dictate what that should be. Your will alone is the determining factor.

"So be sure you have stored good judgment in that portion of the mind which delineates the proposals to you. As mentioned before, it is like a computer — you get out of it what you feed into it. The conclusions you reach are the result of what you have already considered important enough for contemplation. Since thoughts are forms, then the components required for a resolution are already formulated. It remains for you to fit together the pieces. This is accomplished by introspection; with the objective faculties helping to draw out the subjective ideas, which have been implanted beforehand for the purpose of being of some future use. This storehouse is a tool to be used, as we manipulate any instrument to make a construction job more manageable. If the right device isn't utilized, it is because we haven't realized its possibilities.

"Even what we call material items can become more tractable in our hands if we believe in their usefulness. We have proven that all things have a certain degree of activity and reaction to our thoughts. So-called stable chairs and tables, for example, consist of moving atoms and molecules; therefore, we presume even *they* can be responsive to our attitudes toward them. However, we do not 'talk' to them, as we do to a plant or a car that needs attention to prolong its life. But it is a condition that we should keep within our sights: that every particle in our world has a reason for being, and consequently, we should treat each and every one as a part of the entirety, just as *we* are a portion of the Whole."

J have ten typed pages of personal forecasts related to me by mediums, psychics, and teachers. Most have been proven, except those not allowed by time or circumstances. I'll pick out some of specific interest, and begin with those of my Teachers.

January 1974, was the month when all the unexpected things began. First, there was the long communication which I felt compelled to send in to the newspaper. They printed most of it in an article under the heading, "The Other Side." It also gave a summary of my psi experiences, and that I had sent some of my precognitions to the Central Premonitions Registry in New York. This agency studies them and tries to prevent anything which might warn of a future misfortune.

The main idea dealt with the hardships of mankind.

"Plummeting to the depths of despair is unnecessary for the poor of our lands, simply because the rich are hoarding the money and the knowledge they have to correct the situation. This must be stopped, or chaos will result; people — entire regions — will rise up in rebellion.

"The way to prevent this is to educate the masses as to their God-given rights, and how they should go about securing them. There needs to be a Central Citizens' Committee established in each county in the country, to hear and process the grievances of the downtrodden. This should consist of lawyers and ministers who can contribute so much time a week to use their talents to help their fellow man. Then these complaints could be channeled up to the greater offices of the state and the United States. If no action is forthcoming, a higher Citizens' Court ought to be organized to appeal the problems.

"This sounds plausible but seems unlikely to be accomplished? Someone needs to present the idea nevertheless, for the future good of mankind. Accept this challenge to enter the arena of concerned citizens who require a guiding hand, a new concept to which they can attach themselves and raise their sagging hopes for more consideration from the principal sources of government.

"The little man is no longer small in this world. His time

has come to make his voice heard. This should encourage him to do so. Tell it now; do not just wait for those who already realize the sad plight of humanity's inhuman treatment of its own kind."

The "rebellion" has already surfaced — partly in kidnappings and demands of food for the poor. Even our most controversial columnist comments about the poor becoming poorer, the necessity for rearrangement of the country's wealth, or a resulting uprising. These things followed my article. And so, also, did the printed opinion of a man in our area, who wanted to put into practical use what I had stated idealistically. (It was in a different paper.) He had the initiative to try to organize a "Citizens" group to consider the "rights of the people." It almost appears as if the collective unconscious is being contacted in some peculiar way.

I had heard about the Premonitions Registry through a book in which the author told how he had sent them his forecasts. Many of his didn't come true, so it gave me more courage to mail mine to them.

On January 4, 1974, while doing my meditative writing, it was suddenly disclosed: "These things are foreseen for you and the nation: (1) Coming elimination of oil shortage, due to Arabs resuming the supply to U.S. on the third of the month of February. . . ." When this mark was overshot, I requested a recheck and was advised that the date was extended due to some unforeseen circumstances; but it still might have a three in it. On March 13, the Arab oil ministers agreed to lift the oil embargo.

The next one had a less specific date, so could be considered more on target. "(2) The confrontation between Israel and Arabs will end with last firings possible at middle of this month." It was on the 18th of January.

"(3) There will be a bomb explosion in the Washington office of Secretary of State Kissinger when he returns from a trip. It can be found under desk, if room checked carefully."

Again this was one of those partly-right occurrences, because in the same month, but a year later, there was "the explosion of a bomb, causing damage at the State Department. It demolished two offices." Neither office was Kissinger's — but it *was* his department.

On February 19, a few more predictions were slipped to me with the preliminary remark that this was what was viewed as happening soon:

"There is the President's illness, a cause of his leaving

the highest office of the land. This to be before the next year." There seemed to be nothing wrong with his health at that time. Now we know the illness came after he left.

The morning of September 24, I was the recipient of this unexpected disclosure: "Will you be satisfied if you have a worldly revelation given to keep your interest? Because President Nixon waited so long to go to the hospital, he will have trouble regaining his health."

The very next day, the blood clot traveled from his leg and lodged in his lung. The last of October, he had an operation, went into shock, and was in critical condition. Then he contracted pneumonia.

At class the night of November 6, the teacher asked me what I thought Nixon's chances were. I decided to write and find out. "Things look dark for the former President. Only God knows the outcome of this man's life; it hangs by the thin thread of his will to live. There is no reason he'd be taken now."

Evidently his will was strong, as his health continued to improve over the following weeks, and by now he has recovered.

In 1973 I had obtained some notices of national events. There were five of them, inspired by my notice of the *Enquirer's* publication of the winners of their contest. Amateur psychics were to write in what they saw for the year ahead by May; and at the end of December, the letters would be opened and decisions made as to which were most difficult to get accurately.

I missed two completely, but three were so nearly right I thought I might get an honorable mention. It was like nine months of carrying a baby — the suspense of waiting was intolerable. I had alleged that the stock market would rise and fall like mountain peaks. I had also drawn and labeled each point as a month; so it was necessary to check the market pages often to determine if it was going up or down. It conformed to my diagram all but two times, and that may have been owing to my lack of observing it often enough to catch all the variations. Needless to say, this was an aggravation in the year 1973. Besides, someone was more to the point than I was, by noting that the Dow Jones would go below 800. So that left me out on that one.

The earthquake I had forecast for the Los Angeles area in December really happened, but near Laguna Beach, which is south of the big city, of course. The winner had seen 'quakes in or near San Francisco on the date of August 26. Two took place for her, though they were on the first and second of that month.

Then I had said UFO's would be sighted in the states of South Carolina, Georgia, Iowa, and California. These were validated except for Iowa, and I've never read if they were seen there.

I don't think I'll try this long-range angle again. In fact, the prophecy idea really bothers me a bit, because of the accuracy part and having to wait for its outcome. I can see now why I was told: "Yours is not to prophesy, but to tell the truth and banish the lie." While there is a certain satisfaction in knowing someone is helping you give proof of the future to the world, yet the proofs of the Spirit are even more treasured by me. Perhaps I was allowed these few insights in order to realize that they are not really all that important. However, I would like to be useful by counseling individuals some day.

Meanwhile, I'm enjoying the revelations of friends who foresee things for me. They too miss a few here and there, but the ones that hit the target are most outstanding and worthy of note. How to approach all this vast material is the question. The solution may be to go backwards. Not that the recent messages are better, but they may have more general interest, whereas mediums dwelt more on personal memories.

* * * *

Jo is what I call a natural-born psychic, and she was born with a caul, which is supposed to be an indication of this innate ability. We got together about every two weeks, and she told me things that would come up, usually in the near future; and, sure enough, they did. She uses tea leaves as her method of concentration, but the symbols she sees are few, compared to the impressions she receives from some other origin. Her lack of interest in knowing more about this amazes me, as we Geminis are regarded as having an insatiable curiosity.

Jane is also in our sign, and she likes to study the whys and wherefores. She isn't as sure of herself as Jo is, though she is really very good when you can get her to channel. In several cases, she and Jo tuned in to the same incidents, and this was before they had ever met.

I notice that I often have to use my intuition to interpret what might appear to be inconsequential. This episode, forecast by Jo, is an example: "The third Sunday (this turned out to be the third of March and the next day) do not sit too near the front of the church, but in the third or fourth row. You will not like what a speaker says. He will bring a young man with him."

That Sunday Jane and I went up closer to the speaker's platform so I could be sure to hear the special minister for that day. She led the way to the second row, and while I recalled Jo's admonition, I did not remark about it. In front of us was a man with a teenage son. At the night session, he came in late, made disrupting noises with his recorder, and spoke up twice in a way that was displeasing. Not until afterwards did I realize this was the person mentioned. Incidentally, that night I had made a point of sitting in the third row.

Jo declared that a letter was coming from a son. It arrived a week later. I hadn't heard from Terry since his wedding in September, and surely appreciated the December letter. Several months before, she had said, "I see you kissing your son." I dismissed this, because both were so far away in the western states. But on December 13 I had a dream in which this happened. The chance of this imagery being what she foresaw is great, I admit, but I can't deny it either, believing as I do in the divine order of all things, great or small. This is the way I had recorded it: I was walking in the lobby of a big airport. I looked up and saw Terry beside me. I kissed him and said he should have told me he was there. . . . Did I meet him, in dream travel, where he had met us exactly three months before on September 13? And did I somehow convey to him that I wanted him to write? His letter was mailed December 19.

At the end of January, Jo gave me the definite date of February 17 as being a day when I would get news or a package, and a letter about money. On February 18, Terry wrote us from California, included a news article from a paper dated the seventeenth, thanked us for money we had sent, and said they were sending the wedding pictures, which came later — in a package.

Early in the year, Jo had claimed I would take a trip to a church with two persons in two weeks. Three of us had expressed a wish to go to Cassadaga for their Sunday service. But then the driver added another to our group, and also said she would stop at the tavern before the trip home. I was perturbed over this as I knew Gladys had problems with drinking. About a week later, I took a nap and woke up from a dream of being catapulted out of a car, screaming and looking down to see fields beneath me. I thought this might be a subconscious reaction to doubts about riding with Gladys. But it was so frighteningly vivid that I asked Jo's advice about whether I should go. She emphatically stressed that I should not, and to tell the others, as it was a warning. The result was that no one went — a case of free will changing the picture.

Jane's best impression for me was concerning the trip out to Terry's wedding: "The view from the window in Dee's home is bright and beautiful. (I have pictures to prove that — lovely flowers and landscaping.) Avoid Mexican food as could cause upset. (Oddly enough, Terry and Dee took us to just such a restaurant for lunch. Since we'd had three meals on the plane, I had an excuse not to eat any food.) A trip to other areas will insure your seeing places of interest. (We got to do this, especially a tour through a studio.) You can make inquiries about church and people who are like-minded. Try to meet a person who has ESP ability. He will be able to tell things to help you. He doesn't talk to many, but special effort may be made for you to see him. He is thin, white-haired, and youthful in appearance, very wise and sincere, a no-nonsense manner about him. He has a small room for counseling."

The truth of this last was terrific. I was taking lessons from an esoteric study group, which had a church in Los Angeles. I had wanted to talk to the man in charge of it, as I hoped I might be able to actively participate there some day — if I ever got to go out west. It was stated in the pre-lesson material that he could not make appointments to see all the visitors who came. But I wrote ahead anyway and asked for one, quoting what Jean had given me. It proved to be an accurate description. I also sent a writing showing I had done something the lessons had proclaimed was possible. I was told a note about it would help open the door for me, and I guess it did. However, after the interview, I no longer felt that I would fit in with the organization. I don't know if it was his ESP or mine, but I just knew it was not to be.

A woman who had a church and ESP classes gave me a private channeling with these excellent previsions: "You will move soon. I see the number two. You will get a phone call that they have room for you." (The place we wanted was not available, so we found another and moved the second day of the second month of the year. It was also two and a half months after her prediction that we were notified of the vacancy.)

"There will be a trip — a short one, as only two suitcases are visible." (At that time, Tim had not even *met* his future wife. At least he didn't mention it when he was home at Christmas. They were married in March, and we took two bags with us.)

I was asked if my husband was connected with a drafting job. I replied that he had once been with a firm in which his work was related to that department. She said she saw him as smiling over getting back on with them again. (At that time, October 31, 1972, he had no knowledge of any openings. But in February he was interviewed for a position and returned there in March.)

All of these events I've just related were not in any way known by me, so there could have been no possibility of attaining them by telepathy. But even this latter method is valid, in that the clairvoyant can see things not before his physical eyes. I'd like to mention a few of the most evidential facts that Gary was able to glimpse just on the spur of the moment and with his eyes open.

We were talking about some other subject, when he interjected calmly: "You were hit on the nose when a child." (I was struck with a croquet mallet.)

Another time we were chatting in the car outside the church, and he declared that I had a blue bow on some clothing I'd bought. (It was on the seat in a sack.)

"You have an envelope still unsealed, in the shape of a card." (I had purchased one ahead of time for Terry's birthday, which was three months off.)

"There were white pillars on your house. Something is missing at the side." (This was all true, especially about the old elm tree that was finally cut down from the side porch because it was growing too big for the house. This was done after I left.)

"Your piano had arms that curved like a ram's horn, and there was a swivel stool." (This description of the piano was one I'd almost forgotten, but once reminded, it came back to me clearly.)

He discerned my father as having a hearty laugh and wearing a long work apron. The latter was used in his drawing to protect his clothes, and I've always said Dad had a laugh you could hear a block away.

"I see you wading out into the water and shading your

eyes. Your husband walks on ahead, with rolled-up pants, and shoes and socks left behind." (The sun has always bothered my eyes when I'm near the water, and it was a perfect picture of Jay, as he was usually way ahead of me on the beach while I looked for shells.)

This is only a small sample of the verifiable information given to me by many excellent psychics. More could be added, but it would be along the line of Gary's revelations, and I imagine a few consider these less of a manifestation because they could be attained by thought transference. But how many can do this today? Such an elusive thing as two minds getting on the same track still excites me as to our capabilities. Maybe I am too zealous, but anything that proves our intellect can work independently of the physical senses seems worth acclaiming. Accordingly, I will finish with some recent examples of my own insights.

Speaking of sight reminds me of what happened after I'd had mine tested to get new glasses. Following the examination, I came home and lay down to rest my eyes. I began to see things that I assumed were associated with the doctor, since I was thinking about how thorough and careful he had been. I groped for paper and wrote them down. The one I just couldn't believe was seeing him push someone in the face. I was sure he wouldn't admit this, even if he had done it. But he laughingly assured me that this had occurred, and I gathered not just one time!

Other items he didn't recall until I went over the list with him. This lack on the part of the recipients puzzles me, as I've noted it before. Perhaps their memories are recharged by my presence, which acts as a battery.

Out of the many pictures I've seen when I sit under the hair dryer, there was one that must have been precognitive. It was the visualization of a long hospital corridor with a room at the end, which I inferred was a waiting room. I asked the beautician if it had any meaning, but she couldn't place it. That weekend her husband cut his chin and had to have stitches taken in it, after a long "wait" in the emergency room at the end of the hallway of the hospital.

One day I sat down and asked for some provable ideas for Jo. It was the first time I had used the writing method, except for short disclosures. It took me an hour — the length of my customary meditation period. Everything was accurate to at least some degree. I was surprised, Jo was pleased, and even my husband was impressed.

It started out with the statement that these were facts I did not know about Jo, which was evident to both of us.

"She was not good at reading in school — got poor grades." (She said the teacher had to give her extra help so she could get up and read before the class.)

"Purse of silver mesh was a real desire of hers." (Her mother used to make them, and Jo watched in fascination.) "True stories were of interest." (To her mother, she said.)

"Religious background not too much stressed. The family was practical more than prayerful. But she has her own beliefs, and knows she has a gift from God." (She admitted there was not too much attention given to church and religious matters.)

"A locket with pictures has memories." (Jo couldn't recall this, but her husband said her mother had one like that, and it was pinned on her dress.)

"Tunnel ride not enjoyed." (She disliked the enclosed feeling it gave her.) "Beach where had most pleasure." (They weren't too far away from it in New Jersey and she described how she met her husband there.)

"House was a two-story, gray-white color, with a small covered entrance. Trellis had vines — morning glories." (Not much of a porch, and father had enjoyed growing the flower mentioned.)

"Hurt feelings often in childhood. Father was strict but fair. Mother more relaxed." (She said her mother would go to the kitchen and sing when she was angry, instead of saying much.) "Work was paramount in family. No shirking of duties to be performed. Cooperation stressed." (All these points seemed to be accepted by her.)

"Candles used on festive occasions." (Only on birthday cakes.) "Blue one of favorite colors; also indicates healing ability she could develop." (Right on both counts. She told of how a person improved after she touched him.)

There were other times when I got confirmation of things through my writing; though with some, there were clairvoyant or clairaudient experiences first.

The only raps I've had, since I'd ruled them out, occurred one night when I was just going off to sleep. There were three loud ones, a pause, and then two more. I got up groggily and went to the window, where the sounds had come from. I pulled back the curtain and called out, "Yes, what is it? What do you want?"

It was only then that I realized no one could be there, because we were in an upstairs apartment! Even my husband heard it, and he sleeps like a rock. At first he admitted that it was like someone knocking. But then the skeptic took over, and he decided it must have been a backfire. I knew better, but didn't argue the point.

As usual, I sat down with my pencil the next day, and this was verified, along with some added bits of advice:

"The noise was the combined effort of many of us to awaken you to the need to get back to your writing and belief in the power of Spirit. Not spirits, per se, but the wonders of the whole perfect universe that is God's.

"The psychic flower cannot flourish without the watering of the plant. Dryness of the soul produces weakness; it can be kept alive only by more frequent meditation.

"The challenge of being a receiver of our transmission is strong enough to keep you interested for the rest of your years. But the perseverance must be kept at a high pitch. The pursuit of any objective has to be with enthusiasm, or there is a collapse of incentive to see it through."

A short afternoon's sleep ended with a distant ring of a bell, and the sound of my husband clearing his throat. But when I came to complete consciousness, I was aware that the phone could not have rung because I was right by it, and it would have been much louder. Also, Jay was making noises in his sleep, but not like the ones I had noticed. And sure enough, I found out that Spirit had had a hand in it . . . "to make you aware that clairaudience is still possible, even though at the sleep level. Nap times being shorter, it is easier to get evidence to you without disturbing your regular rest hours."

Les, my teacher at one time, had asked me to try for an answer to this ambiguous question: "What can I get from the earth?" The reply was also vague, but it had meaning to him.

"The request of your teacher can be answered in this way: He will reap the fruits of his labors; gold of the kings is his to hold and treasure. But the motives must be respectful of the rights of others. He will know the intent of this."

He affirmed that he was looking for sunken treasure from wrecked ships, and that another man was in it with him, so his rights would therefore have to be considered. I was quite over-whelmed that so much truth had come out of such indefiniteness. On the same day I obtained this information, November 14, I was also told about my husband's chances to get a job . . . He had just been laid off from the company which had rehired him after his return to the Cape. It was quite a shock to us.

A psychic in Orlando had predicted in September that I would be there soon to further my studies. I knew Jay liked it where he was, so I expected it would be years before he would consent to make such a change.

He looked for something for a month in the smaller town. Finally we went over to Orlando, and he was hired as a desk clerk in a motel. We moved on December 14, exactly a month to the day I was given this message: "There will be a try here (in Melbourne) first; then a transfer to the Orlando area. Work at motel good."

While he was applying at one place, I was waiting in the car and reading. I closed my eyes for a few minutes, and viewed a black X over a news advertisement. I felt this indicated he would be turned down . . . and he was. When he had gone to another interview, I placed my pencil on a sheet of notepaper and this was transcribed: "There will be a chance for a job today, though not manifested till later, when he will have a call about it. Move to be about the first week." He was called, accepted employment from this contact, and we moved the second week.

We were taking a trip on the fourth of July. Once again, I was reading and had to rest my eyes by closing them. This strange scene appeared which was puzzling as to its intent: I saw a round, dark hole and pebbles falling into it — like a small sinkhole, I re-marked to Jay.

When we returned home, I was drawn to read a short article, which had the word sinkhole in the headline. I quote it in part:

"A sinkhole in Melbourne that almost claimed the life of a two-year-old girl has been filled . . . [She] fell into it July 4 and had to be revived by her aunt. The hole had been created because city workers were repairing a water main that had been damaged."

If this was more tuning in to the collective unconscious, as propounded by F. W. Myers, then wasn't there a great chance that I might not see the little news item which told about it? Who or what guided me to notice it and thus establish a verity?

A recent dream is worth recording here. In the fall, I revisited the sixty-year-old home where I was born. I not only saw water over the floor, but I could smell gas . . . in the dream. I wrote to Mrs. Lowell about it, and her Christmas card confirmed it: "We have had water come up through the floor in the basement. We also smell gas lots of times . . ."

I don't often interpret other people's dreams, but this one was obvious to me — though not to all the other women who had gathered for a morning coffee. None of them were interested in ESP, I had found out. So when Sara Lee recounted the vision she'd had in her sleep, I blurted out, "I could analyze that, but I think I'll get some more cake instead." I did tell her daughter-in-law about it however, and it was well that I did, for the tragic turn of events would not have been believed by either of us.

Sara Lee had observed herself in a store where they would not take her credit card or a check for the shoes she wanted. Then she found she was outside without any shoes on. . . . There had been much contention over money and property soon to be settled at her son's divorce hearing, and I presumed that the loss of protection (of shoes) referred to that. But the court awarded the largest share to her. However, following the session, she had a stroke and died soon after. She had indeed perceived a great loss.

Helen was an artist who had been in three different classes I had also attended. In October, 1974, she was questioning whether she should keep on with her portrait work, since she wasn't sure it would be lucrative enough. She also wondered if she would achieve any sort of fame with her painting.

I told her I would try to get an opinion in my writing, and this was what was indicated: "Helen is to be famous in this area, and in the field of portrait work especially. She is being inspired by artists from the unseen side of life. But this will not disturb her, because she can comprehend that they are elevated souls. Just as you receive by mind impression, so does she.

"A picture will win award in future show. While money seems important, she must know hers is a gift of God and accept it as such. This means that the inspirational results are of more value than the remuneration."

A year later, after I had moved away, Jane sent me a full-page newspaper article about Helen and her latest award. It was entitled "Portrait of an Artist." She had won a thousand dollars cash prize in the Best of Show category with a picture of her daughter. She had also been given an award as the county's best artist.

The reporter commented about how she caught the "spirit" of people in her paintings, and how she felt guided by a "spiritual essence" in her life. He called her "one of the finest portrait artists in the Southeast."

So Helen had become famous for her portrait work in the area. A picture did win an award in a future show, and she undoubtedly was inspired.

In February of 1975, I was in a new location and hadn't had much opportunity to use my writing in any helpful way. I was advised that I'd be given more confidence if I'd tune in on a neighbor I'd only briefly met. It started with remarks about the daughter who was visiting: "She has problem pertaining to a woman she knows who is interfering in her life. This can be alleviated by a direct confrontation as to course to be taken. Get out of her life! The trip here was wise decision. Better harmony later."

I had a queer feeling that this might refer to Donna's marriage, and hesitated to give the message until I found they all believed in ESP. The daughter said the woman was one she knew at work. But after she returned home, Donna called her mother and revealed that her husband had been seeing another woman for some time. In August Donna got a divorce and now has "better harmony" in her life.

Ellie had moved away from Texas because her husband got work in the East. They were coming down to visit his folks, who lived near us, and I would get to see her. I was going to try a writing for her, but had no idea what day in July she would arrive. On the morning of the seventh, I decided I ought to get busy on the communication for her. Oddly enough, I finished it just a few minutes before she came to the door. It was short, but her comments about it later in November were more lengthy. Since I missed the time element, I wonder if another word should have been inserted. I have put it in parentheses because it seems appropriate, considering what followed.

"Ellie will find a move to be within (sight?) the latter part of the year. Nearer to old place where happier. The job to be type husband had before but with another company. He needs to contact an old friend."

This is what she wrote me at the end of the year: "We had a man from work come over for dinner recently. All day long I thought of the prediction you gave me that Ted needs to contact an old friend . . . about job where we were happier. I knew it was not the guest we were expecting. But, during the course of the dinner the phone rang. An 'old friend' had just flown into town from Texas and wanted to see us. He came over the next night, and it turned out his Dad needed someone in the same type of work Ted did before. The man urged Ted to contact his father, who lives and has his company in Houston — where we want to be! It's not for now, but in the future. He's keeping Ted in mind. This may be the ESP you had. I have great faith in your message! Also, you just didn't know I was coming to your door on that day and hour . . . or that I had moving on the mind!"

To finish off the old year, I was given two more verifiable episodes. One was a brief note: "Hope for the combat between Israel and Arabs ending is useless. The Holy Land will be further desecrated." This was on November 3. Just ten days later the newspaper proclaimed: "A time bomb apparently set by Arab terrorists exploded with a mighty blast in Jerusalem's main shopping street during the evening rush hour . . . killing or injuring more than three dozen persons."

Monday night, December 29, I closed my eyes for a minute and surprisingly visualized a row of bodies covered with dark cloths. The next morning's paper disclosed that eleven were killed in the bomb blast of an airport in New York City. There was also a picture of several bodies laid out in a row. It happened the same night I saw it, and I wish I had recorded the time, so I would know if it was precognition or postcognition. This is a case that proves we should never forget to keep complete records.

At the same Kennedy Airport, on November 13 in 1975, a DC-10 was wrecked after birds were sucked into the engine. I'd had a dream in September that I was on a runway at an airport. Birds were on it, and I tried to sweep them off with a stick.

This example, as well as others, raises the question: if I had been able to get the exact location and time and reported it, is there a chance it could have been prevented? But also, if the event was seen so far ahead, does it mean it would happen anyway? This could start a debate about predestination, which I do not really believe in, because anything can be changed by our free will. The problem is to get the skeptics to listen to warnings. Having a well developed intuition helps some to sense when to avoid these disasters. But unfortunately not too many have raised their consciousness to this level.

April 5, 1976, I had closed my eyes to exclude the commercials which came on before the newscast at 5:30. What I visualized had no immediate transpiring, so I forgot about it — though I did record the date and time and told Jay about it. There was a yellow school bus near an overpass. I thought it must be involved in an accident, because it was turned sideways and not going under the structure.

On May 21, a school bus crashed through a guard rail on a highway near San Francisco. It was pictured in the paper as I'd seen it — in front of the overhead freeway and turned parallel to it. I had viewed it as upright in my mind's eye, but I wouldn't have been able to tell what it was if it had been on its top and crushed. No time was given, but it was reported on the late afternoon news — at 5:30 — and I just happened to be watching it, as I had done a month and a half before.

We got to know a young sheriff's deputy through Jay's job of night security at the park where we were staying. I found out that Perry had an interest in ESP so I decided to try a writing for him. I had done it only now and then, and was doubtful that it would be accurate. But I was only one day off on one thing. Since he was a lawman, I had some trepidation about the whole idea . . . and more relief than usual over its ultimate truth.

"Monday was the day the deputy was married. (Sunday was correct. Maybe I hadn't quite reached my alpha level on the first sentence!) Religion is Methodist. (Though he had changed religions, he did return to the one of his original upbringing.) He is one of four children — not all lived. (The number was right; and his mother informed him she had lost a baby, as his wife had recently.) Electrical work he likes to do; also read and talk to people. (I wasn't sure of the reading, since he was in such an active profession, but he admitted to this enjoyment, as well as the others.)

"Some things only he would know: The most idiotic incident regarding work was that time when a woman tried to make love to him. (I was naturally reticent over having to reveal this to him, but he smilingly conceded this had happened.) He was injured on a bicycle when a child. (I was shown the large, white scar that resulted from this.) Two times he hit a playmate when accosted first unjustly. (I was assured that this had indeed happened.)

"He will be getting more money soon in some way.

(Courses he is taking will lead to an increase in pay.) The next child will be a boy — this one will live — so follow doctor's advice. (I hope to keep in touch to find out if this comes true.) Approach cars with caution in the next few months — someone will be armed." (I hadn't expected confirmation on this so soon, but a week later, Perry told Jay that there was an incident with a car in a robbery. Details not to be told.)

"This will be a good year for work and home life." (That must have made him feel better about the dangers of his work in a profession that is all too little appreciated.)

* * * *

The proofs have been given; the messages related. Yet the supply is inexhaustible, and the truths will forever be unfolded. We are assured that as He could do, we can do also. There is realization of the many hazards in our way toward attaining the heights. That is why we are presented with an endless opportunity to elevate . . . in this life and the next.

The other dimension also offers chances to develop, which may seem an incredible idea to those who think it is only a place of rest. But as we have tried to picture it, learning continually goes on.

And, moreover, you can still gain the gifts of the Spirit here and now. No matter what your age, it is your privilege to know and be taught. So unlock the door — you have the key — for, as you have seen, there is no end.

ABOUT THE AUTHOR

Clare A. Clark is a determined woman, convinced that, through her psychic powers, she can be of real service to humanity's continuing interest in what the future holds; and in establishing a closer communion with the Higher Source.

It began eight years ago when she took a course in parapsychology. "A door began to open," she says. "I started to have dreams that came true, and some even became predictions of future happenings."

Her main interest, however, is inspirational writing, which interprets problems for friends, or dreams that are not clearly understood.

Clare was an art teacher for seven years, has a major in English, and has written poetry and short stories. She lived in one house and one town for half her life before marrying a Navy photographer. They are still traveling, even though he has retired from the service. Her studies in psychic development have taken her throughout central Florida.

In this, her first book, she demonstrates not only clarity of expression, but also an uncanny ability to make a real believer of her reader. This combination of writing skills makes for an absolute spellbinder from start to finish.

ABOUT THE BOOK

This book expresses the theme that our lives never end, nor do our spiritually-attained psychic abilities. It is a well-organized, convincing work, which will stir both the inspiration and imagination of its readers.

The first sections describe how the author's study began, and we are introduced to the author's own experiences with the senses of smell, touch, and hearing, and how she interpreted them.

Clairvoyance, dreams, and almost unbelievable transmissions from "The Other Dimension" which the author has received are explored in great depth.

Then the reader is led into the subject of reincarnation, as well as some very unusual "far-out" stories that include such things as UFO contact, The Devil's Triangle, a return from spirit, and mind control. God as spirit, prayer, the soul, meditation methods, and color meanings are dealt with in a way which captivates the readers and makes them think of their own beings, pondering how these subjects may apply to *them.*

The book concludes with the author's ideas on the metaphysical subject of "truth"; and her own predictions which have come true.